Retirement FOR BEGINNERS

DO IT RIGHT THE FIRST TIME

A Personalized How-To Book of Choices and Ideas if You are Thinking About or are Already Retired

CARMA LOU RICH-SAATHOFF

INKWATER PRESS

PORTLAND • OREGON

Copyright © 2005 by Carma Lou Rich-Saathoff

Cover and interior designed by Masha Shubin

All rights reserved. No part of this book may be reproduced or transmitted in any form or by any means whatsoever, including photocopying, recording or by any information storage and retrieval system, without written permission from the publisher and/or author. Contact Inkwater Press at 6750 SW Franklin Street, Suite A, Portland, OR 97223-2542.

www.inkwaterpress.com

ISBN 1-59299-122-X

Publisher: Inkwater Press

Printed in the U.S.A.

DEDICATION

For my Boomers –

Bill and Georgia, Leslie and Brent, Kim, Irv Bob and Merrillee, Teresa and Bill, Jim, and never to be forgotten Bob

TABLE OF CONTENTS

Author's Notes vii

Introduction xi

Moving Criteria 1
    Location Options 3
    Choosing a Location 8
    The Biggest Yard Sale 13
    Finding a Place to Live and Making it Yours 17
    Budgeting 30

Settling In 37
    Getting Involved 39
    Making New Friends 47
    Dating Do's & Don'ts 55
    Odds 'n Ends Tidbits Leftovers
        Miscellaneous Wants and Needs 62
    Mates and Partners 68

Appearance 79
    Wardrobe 81
    Hair & Make-Up 91
    Birthday Underwear 97
    Cosmetic Surgery 101

Eating Plans 105
    Information 107
    Dieting 109
    Lou's Sample Meals 111
    Keeping It Off 114
    Staying Trim 121

Health 125
    Medical Thoughts 127
    Mental Health 135
    Unkind People 139
    Changes or How I Have Changed 143

Sex 149
    Looking Forward to Sex 151

Conclusion 165
    Conclusion 167
    Addages, Aphorisms
        & Bon Mots 169
    Explanation & Cover Letter 173
    Questionnaire 177

AUTHOR'S NOTES

"It's not whether you win or lose, but how you play the game"

Several friends had suggested that I write a book about my experiences and education as a retiree. They were impressed with how I adjusted after I left the town where I was so settled into my life as wife and business owner, and started over alone in a new community. And not only that but I seemed so happy and satisfied with my new life. They never thought I would leave the contented and secure existence that I had struggled to achieve and now I appeared to have found even more happiness. Each one asked the same questions and they all started with Why? and/or How?

After much thought and urging via e-mail from the most persistent and positive friend I have, Dr. Marta Mooney of Fordham University, I decided to give it a shot and write the book. I hope the result will help you in thinking about options you have, and in making decisions about situations that may have arisen or might arise in your retirement years. I make no pretense of being an authority on everything, or even anything, for that matter. None of us knows it all, but it is easy to forget much that we have learned, so just read & enjoy & maybe enrich your lives.

When I was still thinking about the book, I thought it would be great to have feedback from various friends from around the country so I devised a five-page questionnaire with an explanatory cover letter. My purpose with the anonymous answers was to give examples of how other people handled the same problems in other ways and also to back up my experiences with the ideas of others. I wrote the book first, then read the questionnaires, and then inserted the quotes and ideas from those pages.

I gave that packet to many friends here in town. Then I got out my address book and mailed over 100 inquiries to seniors I know all over the country. While in the process of writing, I always carried questionnaires with me so I could hand them out to a likely respondent. I have added the questionnaire to the back of the book and I welcome you to fill it out and send it to me. Who knows maybe I will do a revised edition or sequel down the road and your thoughts will be included.

And speaking of feed back I have some people to thank. First. Marta Mooney for her continuous and enthusiastic support for this project. I have known this woman for 40 years and she has never strayed from her goals or her friends. And thank you to Carolyn and Vick Knight of Canyon Lake, California. They both are authors/writers aand Vick is a wine columnist for the Riverside Press-Enterprise. Their technical know-how, suggestions, and generous and knowledgeable advice have been invaluable to me for 20 years. I must thank retired law Professor Richard Tench for his belief in my talent and me. He has never wavered in his confidence and I only have to give him one or two glasses of apple juice a week for his support. And

Pam Treves is so full of thoughts & ideas and is always willing to share. As a retired Hospital Administrator and Mediator, she has lots of information. Noma Tracy Childs was invaluable to me when I moved and as a morale booster. And there is Diana Mati, my computer mentor. I absolutely could not have put it together without her generous assistance. Bouquets to each of you. I must express my overwhelming gratitude to my friends, pals, buddies & acquaintances for their time & contributions to my questionnaire. Thank you!!

And one last word of appreciation to my Grandma and my Mom & Dad for the lives they led that have inspired me these many years. And especially for the adages, bon mots, and aphorisms that are timeless and caught me in my tracks many times over the years. My Dad ended all of his letters to me, "D L T B G Y D" and I haven't. Thanks Dad!

INTRODUCTION

"A job worth doing is a job worth doing well"

When you write an article or a book you have to choose your audience. My thought was who is going to read this thing? I originally thought to gear it to people in their late 50's or early 60's. People who are starting to think about their future or maybe realize their total lack of plans for this coming wonderful time in their lives. And then I thought what about those other seniors who are just plugging along or (heaven forbid) only boringly passing time until they die. For those of you over that age there's a lot in here for you to learn, think about, and consider. This book has turned out to be for all of us "soon to be old people, in-between-people, seniors, retirees', etc. For you this is a book about choices. So often it is that one idea around the corner that can change your path.

In this book, I discuss Choosing a New Location and the criteria I used, Making It Yours no matter where, plus other options to consider. I talk about why I chose this Kind of Residence to live in and mention other possibilities. There's a chapter on Making New Friends, Keeping Old Ones, and a section on Getting Involved in Life that goes side by side with Senior Organizations, part time jobs and volunteering.

I talk about Money and Budgeting and sacrifices and pleasures and making it all work for the person you are. There is a too long section, but oh so useful, on Eating Plans, getting there and staying that way as long as possible. You are still in charge.

There are bits here and there on entertainment and how to enjoy what's there for you. The chapters on Mates and Partners, Dating Do's and Don'ts bring you into the 21st Century. It is different whether you are with someone, and really different when you are alone.

Being involved, interesting and informed is also important and included in various sections along the way.

How about your Wardrobe and Appearance and Hair? Make sure all you Males read these hints. I share with you my limited knowledge on Cosmetic Surgery as well as observations on Make-Up disasters. One may wonder why I have used a couple of chapters on total Appearance. Because there is more to a good life when you're retired and not working than just moving and getting settled. It is all important.

There are chapters on Medical Health, Mental Health and finding good care in a strange place. And have you known Unkind People that unfortunately are part of your daily life and must be dealt with too often? There are suggestions included.

And nearly last, a segment I called Looking Forward to Sex. Those feelings and urges never really go away and here are some ideas, thoughts and experiences that you may not have associated with your retirement. That's why "Retirement for Beginners" is for you.

The last chapter is about Mental, Emotional and Intellectual Changes that happen to us.

A mother in law in my family summed it up with this quote, "Life's journey is not to arrive at the grave safely in a well preserved body, but rather to slip in sideways, totally worn out, shouting, "Holy shit! What a ride!"

MOVING CRITERIA

"To thine own self be true"

LOCATION OPTIONS

"There's more than one way to skin a cat"

Unless you stay in the same home or condo or whatever, you probably are going to move to a smaller place. And that's OK. We all accumulate so much stuff and eventually some one has to deal with it. It's your stuff; you should decide what is to become of it. But first you have to make the big decision. Where am I going to live?

There are so many options to consider. There are retirement condos & co-ops all over the country with golf courses, tennis courts, racquet ball, and so forth. They are lovely and guarantee that you can do all those things if that is your choice. I know many people who have been waiting all their working years to play golf or tennis seven days a week if they feel like it. And more power to them. If you choose this option, you will meet many people doing exactly what they want and you have an excellent opportunity to make lots of new friends. Enjoy! And keep your head down.

The option that I wanted to choose was to put all our worldly goods in storage, or else rent the house furnished, and take off for a few years. My idea was to live in London, Paris, Rome, and Madrid each for six months so that I would feel I really knew the place. New York, Washington D.C., Chicago, Seattle, Los

Angeles, San Francisco were next in line after Europe. Who knows I may have eventually expanded my list to include Toronto, Tokyo, Singapore, Melbourne, and Honolulu to name a few.

I mentioned six months, and it could be four, but definitely plan a lengthy stay in each City if you decide to do this. What a wonderful way to learn about a place and to be able to feel at home by knowing your way around and to enjoy the many possibilities each City and culture has to offer. I had hoped to rent a furnished place for that length of time.

Doesn't it sound like a great idea? Well, my moving away from my husband put a halt to those dreams. But that doesn't mean you can't try it! Let me know how it goes!

I know two women who for reasons of their own just decided there's more to life than this little town or city where they lived. One had an ongoing love for a certain location and the other just wanted a drastic change to her boring routine. They read books, wrote the Chamber of Commerce in various places and studied everything they could before making a decision. I'm happy to report that Honolulu and Montana suit them to a tee.

Some of my friends have made "the big decision" before retirement and moved into a smaller place before they retired. They got a lot of problems out of the way while their life was still as it always was. Often their families are in the same vicinity and there is no good reason to move and lots of reasons to stay. That is wonderful. Shirley and Roger did the above and their plan is to get in the car and drive all over the country visiting friends in all the spots they have chosen. That sounds like a great idea to me! I'm looking forward to their visit.

I know other couples, while still employed, who each year on their vacation go visit a spot that they are interested in and stay for a while to learn about it. Weather, prices, affordability, etc. I think that is one of the smart ways to choose a new spot. You will see what you're getting into if it is a place you have only heard about. Now you'll know for sure.

Before I forget an interesting thought: There are about eight states that do not have personal income tax! Those states are: Alaska, Florida, Nevada, New Hampshire, South Dakota, Texas, Washington, Wyoming. However, in New Hampshire you pay state tax only on Interest & Dividend income. Now all this is something to consider. There are other states that do not have sales tax which is another option to consider. Do investigate. It may help you decide.

This seems a good place to mention Elderhostel. Get on their mailing list and visit some of the spots you are curious about before you retire. As a single senior female, I have found Elderhostel to be the perfect solution to my travel worries. They take care of everything and I am free of those stressful burdens. Each trip I have taken has resulted in meeting someone who became a good friend. The couples and singles are there because they want to be. The prices are very reasonable. The travelers impressed me as intelligent, interested in learning, and delighted with the opportunities that Elderhostel offered. This is a wonderful chance for you to visit places where you might be interested in living.

Other friends have always wanted to live in the desert or in Florida. Charleston or Savannah are lovely cities that could be considered. Parts of Mexico are very desirable, as is Hawaii. Those are wonderful spots and have much to offer seniors.

Rancho Bernardo (part of San Diego) and Palm Springs are lovely as are the various Sun Citys around the Southwest. If you love the East, you might consider Toronto, Portland, Maine, Cape Cod and of course Boston or Providence. In the Southwest there is Albuquerque, Phoenix, Mesa and Las Vegas to consider. In the Northwest there is Puget Sound, Seattle, Vancouver and Victoria in Canada. There are college towns that abound with culture and opportunities, like Walla Walla, Washington, which has three colleges. I have visited many of my friends over the years around the country and what delightful lives they have made for themselves in new and different environments. Their contentment is apparent.

The 2003 summer issue of AARP had a wonderful section that they suggested as "Best Places to Retire". Their criteria included available jobs, affordable housing, culture & entertainment, outdoor recreation, a feeling of safety for persons and property, college or university, a sense of community, proximity to health care, good public high schools, and last but far from least good transportation. Excellent!

The cities they recommend in alphabetical order by state:
1. Fayetteville, Arkansas
2. San Diego, California
3. Loveland / Fort Collins, Colorado
4. Gainesville, Florida
5. Sarasota, Florida
6. Iowa City, Iowa
7. Portsmouth, New Hampshire
8. Asheville, North Carolina
9. Santa Fe, New Mexico

10. Ashland, Oregon
11. Charleston, South Carolina
12. San Antonio, Texas
13. Bellingham, Washington
14. Spokane, Washington

So there are some more options to choose from. Have fun and enjoy your travels.

And everyone seems to want to take advantage of the opportunity to travel. Go for it. And please, get a good passport photo. A few words about packing. Choose two main colors and accessories that will mix and match with either color. The old adage, "put out everything that you want to take, then take half as many clothes and twice as much money" is still pretty good advice. Another good idea is to take your medications & prescription copies in your carry-on, along with your jewelry, address book, make-up and a toothbrush. Some people prefer to put their medications in the small 1 ½ inch Zip-Loc bags for ease in handling. When packing your carry-ons or other baggage for commercial traveling, remember not to put any sharp objects into your carry-ons, including your purse, fanny pack or back pack. You know why.

CHOOSING A LOCATION
"Think positive"

I think what you have to do before you even consider choosing a location is to think about you: your roots, your hobbies, your health, your needs, your family, your friends and so on. Write down, make a list of your needs, necessities, wants & desires and anything else you can think of that has to do with you and your life. Then, cull it down, and make a list of the important things that a location must provide. Notice the phrase is "must provide". Ask yourself all these questions, and you might consider asking some of your family or friends for suggestions about your needs. Whether they are worthwhile or make an impression is up to you. But, one never knows when a good idea may pop up!

I had been with the love of my life for 28 years but when our lives together changed in a negative direction, I decided I had to get out and move away. All of that is not pertinent to this book except for the fact that at 66 I moved to a city 1000 miles away, knowing only one person there and started over. I mean over from scratch. My friend, Tracy and her husband moved away after about six months so she hasn't been here as I have settled in but she knew me so well and got me off to a great start. I'm ever grateful.

I grew up in Des Moines, which to me has always been a City. It had live theatre, amateur theatre, movies downtown and in the neighborhoods, an art museum, lots of restaurants, a fine newspaper, Better Homes & Gardens is published there, libraries, 7 or 8 high schools, Drake University, 3 country clubs, private dining clubs, many churches, is a huge insurance center and has a good transportation system. I traveled on those trolleys and streetcars as a youngster going to the dentist, to a part-time job and to school and other places at times. I really liked and took advantage of City living as a youngster. Hey, sounds like a great place to live! It is! And I recommend it highly to anyone looking for a healthy City in the Midwest. I have been gone 50 years and a wise old owl once said, "You can't go home again". However, there are lots of people out there who would find Des Moines the perfect location for their retired years. I have friends from long ago who have stayed and are as content as anyone could be.

While a stewardess for UAL I lived on the Peninsula near San Francisco. Near but not there. With my husband and children, I moved further into the suburbs and lived in various towns in the area for 30 years. Eventually I remarried, and later we moved to Lake Elsinore in southern California. I realized I was totally dependent on a car and eventually I determined that when I moved, I wanted to live in a City again. I struggled with myself to make crucial decisions. To enjoy the rest of my life and what it had to offer was my main goal. Not to be dependent on a car became a large and important financial part of that goal

When I decided to move I listed all the cities in the world that I would be interested in. This then was my criterion for making a choice:
1. Affordability
2. Weather/climate
3. Culture availability
4. Transportation and
5. Accessibility to family.

I want to explain about #5. My children have their own lives as I do. They have lived many miles from me since they grew up and so for many years we have become used to being apart. As it turned out, Colorado and southeast Washington aren't that far from Portland and I see them usually at least once a year. If there were an emergency my son, Bill, could be here rather quickly. We talk on the phone and we e-mail whenever we want. So I don't feel detached from them. My son drives 4 hours once a year for a couple of days visit and I rent a car and do the same to visit his houseful of 4 teen-agers and his very patient, lovely wife! My daughter, Leslie, flies to see me from Colorado once a year or I go there. I really haven't ever felt isolated or cut off from my children. I feel we are all comfortable with the arrangement. And that's important. We don't need family worrying about us when it isn't necessary. Later on is fine but not when all is going well. Some Seniors feel that their children's overly being concern is butting in and they aren't ready to give up their independence or their privacy yet. Don't you agree?

As you can imagine the list of criteria eliminated a lot of possibilities. For my income, San Francisco, New York too expensive, Denver & Chicago too cold, London, New York & D.C. too far away, Seattle, San Diego and Los Angeles too spread out.

I chose Portland. It is not for everyone. It is a big City and spread out but yet feels condensed because of its brilliant transportation system. Lots of people complain about the weather and I say, "Move". Why spend your remaining years complaining about the weather, for Pete's Sake? To me, it's only weather. And it does rain as advertised. I bought a blue, with black trim, rubberish raincoat, some black rubber shoe/boots that I can wear with almost anything, and a big black rain hat. I tromp all over in that outfit. I can even splash in the puddles like Gene Kelly and I often do just that. I also have a couple of umbrellas that I carry" just in case" on other days when it might rain. I have a black one for winter and a yellow one for the Spring and Summer. Portland is not for everyone, but it is for me.

Whether or not you have a car, you should be walking more these years. Think of that when choosing a spot in which to settle. Be close enough to the store, drugstore, and cleaners so they are convenient and that you can walk to the library, post office, and maybe a mall or at least, some shops. Find out where the bus stops or where other public transportation is. How about your church, synagogue or mosque? My goal was to move, get settled, and not have to move again. I wanted to establish a social base for these remaining years and be comfortable with a different medical group. Anyway, think about it all and be aware of these advantages as you will grow older and maybe won't be driving a car anymore at all.

How can I explain the feelings I had once I unpacked and settled in? I was so lucky. I honestly felt instantly at home. I don't know why. Maybe because my Dad was born in the Northwest or maybe because I was friendly and the people reciprocated. But I was comfortable. I had decided beforehand that if it didn't work after a decent interval that I would move on. But that never was even a consideration. My advice is: Don't be afraid, do it. It's your life and the only one you have so don't waste precious time, energy & money being miserable.

THE BIGGEST YARD SALE

"Honesty is the best policy"

It took us weeks to get our yard sale ready. There's a lot of emotional baggage involved and you need to take the time to deal with all of it. That beautiful bowl that belonged to Aunt Stella is never going to be used, so maybe you should part with it. The same for that power lawn mower. It ain't easy but has to be done.

Something I did was call a Collectibles Shop that I trusted and asked the owner to come out to the house and tell me what she would give me for the bigger collectible pieces and some antiques. I'm talking about the really good stuff that shouldn't sit in the yard and most people wouldn't pay what it was worth at a yard sale but would in a shop. She did and we bargained after she gave me the grand total and we both walked away happy. Me, because I didn't have to deal with it anymore and I certainly got more than I paid for anything and she, because she got a hell of a deal. It was worth it!

There are a couple of ways to go here with the rest of the stuff. Where to do this is your next big problem. Garages are never big enough if you are truly getting rid of everything that you won't need in that condo or apartment or any other retirement residence. Use the garage & driveway (if it doesn't rain) for all the garage stuff and everything from the yard, porch, patio etc. Then clear out the living room of what you are keeping (hopefully, you're selling the couch & that ugly huge lounger), put all the tables you can find in there and start putting the stuff out. I used the dining room table, book cases, a desk, end tables and coffee tables, everything. Then arrange your stuff in some semblance of order. Pots & pans & kitchen stuff together, books, jewelry, clothes & shoes, bedding, pictures, all grouped together by category.

After everything was spread out I just left it there for a few days to contemplate. After all, this was my life and part of my deceased parents life that I was parting with and I had to be certain I would never want that particular little odd thing again. If your kids live near by, they will probably want everything. That's your problem and decision. I can't help you to deal with that. Naturally, we did change our minds about some things and as it turned out, added some things we had originally decided to keep. I still regret getting rid of my zippered navy blue boots. Don't let anyone rush you here because this is important for the next 30 or so years of your life. (Item: keep that file cabinet) If you are in doubt, keep it. There are no tomorrows here.

You need to plan ahead for when you want this major week-end to be, then back track on the calendar and write down when you are going to do what. Take your time. It is a very tiring and exhausting task, chore, job, whatever. So don't kill yourself before the big week-end. Save up paper & plastic bags for the customers. I had some easy to carry boxes for them to use as they were shopping. Oh, and here's a biggie: Decide if you want to let dealers come a day early. They will try to talk you down on everything. I say No.

You have to write an ad for every newspaper in the area. They will come from miles around for your Estate Sale and that is what I would call it. Don't chintz on the ad. It is the only thing you are doing to get people there besides a big cardboard sign in the front.

OK so everything is laid out and you have to price it. How do you know what to ask for anything? Before you start any of this procedure and during the sorting, etc. go to other yard sales in the neighborhood. Visit second hand stores and collectible shops. Compare and then you can price accordingly. Be prepared to bargain. Don't price too low. But remember why you are doing this: To Get Rid of It All! Sunday afternoon is bargain time. I had one man who so wanted a certain antique dining table and we couldn't agree on a price on Saturday so I told him that if it wasn't sold by Sunday afternoon, he could have it at his price. He agreed. But I sold it before he returned. On a desk we were getting rid of, I did the same thing and when the man returned, he got the desk.

My suggestion about the money is quite simple. Bill & I both wore fanny packs for the money. We kept the money for making change and some small bills for the same thing in one compartment and then periodically we would separate the bigger bills and stash them in a different section of the fanny pack. That way the customers do not see the big wad that you eventually accumulate. You will have to use your own judgment about accepting checks. Getting ATM cash is so easy, I suggest cash only unless you know the person.

Our sale started at 8:00 a.m. on Saturday and there were people outside at 7:00 waiting for the big event. We were smart and had put a barricade up that said something sweet like "Wait 'til 8:00". Thank goodness. We were still eating at 7:00 & it was going to be a long, long day. Bill handled the garage and yard stuff while I stayed in the house with those things. My daughter came from Colorado to help and to claim part of her inheritance. You do need that extra help because there are a lot of people and money coming & going and someone needs to be "in sight on site" at all times. We also placed two of the older grandchildren here and there, helping both grandpa and me. It really was a fun time for the whole family in spite of the long hours on our feet.

When it was all over we had sold everything except for two paintings we had priced too high. In retrospect, I think we did that on purpose. We were happy to keep them and delighted with the success of our sale. We were totally pooped but not too tired for us all to go out for dinner and have champagne all around!

Or you can forget all of the above and hire a professional Estate Sale person to organize and handle everything. And I mean everything. It isn't cheap but sometimes it is worth the cost if you don't have the time, energy or inclination. Choices, choices, choices!

FINDING A PLACE TO LIVE AND MAKING IT YOURS

"You can do anything if you just set your mind to it"

I have never, ever, ever lived by myself. It was such a big undertaking and one that I never thought I would do. But life goes on and fate takes a hand now and then. All old clichés, but oh! so pertinent. I was lucky to have one friend in my City of choice.

When I called Tracy in Portland to tell her I was moving, she said, "Well, c'mon up for a week. Stay with us and we'll find you a place. When are you coming? And when are you moving?" Whatta friend!

Their apartment was in a big high rise 21 blocks from downtown. I had never been in one and was immediately enchanted. I adore Tracy but felt it best not to live in the same building. I would rely on her too much and not do stuff on my own. We had lived around the corner from each other two other times and that was convenient enough. We wanted to be close but not in each other's way. That was my goal.

We found another high rise around the corner in the same neighborhood and I rented an apartment on the 9th floor. I had 500 sq. ft. and a view of Mt. St. Helen's. I was 18 blocks from town, 4 blocks from the grocery store, and 2 blocks from City buses. It was all very convenient after I learned a few things.

I signed a year's lease that started in one month and said, "I'll see you July first".

There is a bright clean laundry room on the first floor. I brought my iron but not the ironing board so I suggested to Jay, the manager, that it would be nice and so convenient if the building furnished an ironing board for tenants. Jay thought it a good idea and did it. He even bought an iron that we can borrow. Also in the laundry room is a big shelf for people to pass on their hand-me downs. Isn't that great? I got a beautiful black rayon blazer, a couple blouses, some fantastic sweaters, and four nifty baskets. My neighbor picked up some wineglasses and a serving platter. You have to love freebies.

We have a pleasantly decorated Community Room that is used for all sorts of things besides having our mailboxes. There are tables and chairs and an attractive kitchen, which is the center of management sponsored parties for the tenants on occasion. What I love about the Community Room is it is a place for tenants to leave their magazines and books for others to use and enjoy. I love the recycling. The room is a lovely spot to meet your neighbors and to sit and chat for a while. There is also a chess board table and a drawer full of jigsaw puzzles.

Tracy was very smart and knew me so well. She told me to get an apartment above the tree line (7th floor). She pointed out that I am an outdoor, sunshine person and on the lower floors it is often gray, cloudy and depressing. Tracy told me to keep the shades up and it will be bright on even the gloomiest of days. And she was so right! I have never felt depression when I was feeling blue, lonesome or sad. It's too damn bright! Now I keep the blinds down but the slats wide open. It's bright, but comfortable, not blinding!

I have to talk about security. When I was 16 I had a bad experience walking home from work during the Christmas holidays. It left me scared and super cautious. I do not go out at night alone and it is imperative that I feel secure in my home. Believe me living on the 9th floor was about the most secure I could feel. Plus there is a security guard on patrol all night long. And it is a secure building with locked doors and buzzers and all that paraphernalia. Thank goodness. Remember this if you have pangs of fear as I do. "Better safe than sorry".

There are 190 units in this building and I have lived in three different apartments in the five years I have lived here. First I moved more to the front, and then to a view unit with a terrace and a fireplace. I was so very lucky as most apartments don't have balconies; often it is only condos that do. I have made many friends here in the building and still love it. I am grateful to my old friend, Tracy, every day for her friendship and encouragement. I have tried to emulate those qualities and found it very satisfying.

When I decided I wanted to live in a City with good transportation. I also made the decision not to have a car. It costs between $65 and $100 a month to rent parking space in almost any building. You can get a street parking permit for various amounts starting at $25 a year. Add auto insurance, gas and maintenance and you have quite a monthly expenditure out of your retirement income. Parking downtown is outrageous. I left the car with my husband and have been walking healthily ever since. When I visit the kids in Walla Walla I rent a car. Cheap compared to a years' expense for just one or two car trips annually. A lot of my friends have cars and sometimes we do things together like shopping at Costco with Kathy or going for a

River Walk in Vancouver with Pat. But when we go to the movies or the library or out to lunch or dinner, we walk. It all works out just fine.

I knew that once I got back to my home in California and started trying to decide what to take for my first apartment, it would prove to be a horrendous task It was amazing how it turned out. I even fooled myself. First, I took very careful measurements of each room, closet, nook & cranny and drew it on an open manila folder 1/4 inch to a foot scale. Then when I got home I cut out little bits of green cardboard for the furniture I wanted to bring to the same 1/4 inch scale. With that done I was able to play house with the floor plan and the furniture pieces. Bill & I discussed what furniture he wanted and what I wanted and then played with the pieces to decide if they fit. It was a simple plan and saved me lots of hassle. The movers were delighted when they arrived in Portland and I knew exactly where every thing belonged. It was a breeze and I highly recommend it.

Three years later when I got my latest and last apartment with its outdoor space, I needed plants, containers, table & chairs, etc. Bill wasn't going to want half the stuff we had accumulated when he moved to Texas the following year, and told me to take what I wanted. That's when we decided to have the Estate Sale the next year when we both knew for certain what we were each going to need and want.

My neighbor, Mary, and I drove a Hertz rent-a-truck up to Portland from Southern California. We filled the truck with all the stuff that I could possibly use and off we went. It was a wonderful experience and one that I would do again. The truck was comfortable and handled so well for a novice truck driver.

You could do it if you had to and tried. It was great. Mary was also amazed at the ease of handling this 14' truck. Afterwards a package arrived in the mail from Mary's husband. It contained a T-shirt that showed a truck and driver with "Mary & Lou" on one line and "Mother Truckers" on the other!

A few things that I learned along the way. So much new furniture of today is bulky and huge, and rooms in apartments and condos are usually not large. The end result is a lot of that style furniture isn't going to look right in an apartment. Big furniture makes the rooms look dinky. Your rooms will look so crowded you will be unhappy. I get so disgusted with designers of furniture. What is this big stuff and where is it going to fit? Jessica McClintock has a new line of furniture that is smart, good looking and suitable for any place you choose to live, well, except for a log cabin in the woods. If you're buying new, check it out.

My Dad had a small, but cozy lounge chair that was the perfect size for me and suitable for any room. I kept it and had it recovered in an off white fabric and it's gorgeous. Or it was. It's been five years and I think I will do that one chair over in off white leather because I sit in it every night and no matter how careful I am, it is getting soiled and tacky. I even put a big beach towel on it in the summer to protect the upholstery from natural skin oils but it doesn't do any good. I have light colors and I refuse to upholster it in dark colors just so it looks clean.. Doesn't that sound just like a woman? Well, I am and it's OK. It's my chair! Light leather upholstery seems to be the answer.

About dishwashers and that wonderful convenience when you had a family. Well, if you are alone, you just don't need one. They take up valuable cupboard space or floor space if it is a portable and you live in an apartment. I had them take my portable out as well as the stack washer & drier in the kitchen. I needed that space for shelves and a portable cabinet that I brought from my house. There is a big laundry room in the building that I use every two weeks and only on weekdays. The working people don't need us retirees using those machines on the only days they have off. How would you feel? It's kinda A Golden Rule thing.

More on you being the dishwasher. I wash my dishes once a week or whenever I run out of plates or silverware. When I am through cooking something, and before I eat, I clean out any pots or pans, salad bowl, baking dish, whatever & let them dry while I eat. When I am through eating, I rinse & stack the dishes in a neat pile as well as the silverware. I put away the dried pots, etc., wipe up the counter and I'm through for that meal. Believe me, it really works and actually doesn't make me antsy about the mess in the kitchen. There is no mess in the kitchen. It's just a neat pile of rinsed dishes waiting their turn. (And I save on dishwashing detergent. Every bit helps.)

One more thing about dirty glasses. I put all glasses and cups used by my guests in the pile with the other dirty dishes. My juice glass used each morning is rinsed out thoroughly and placed upside down on the rim of the sink to dry out. I do the same with my wineglass. My water glass and my drink-before-dinner glass have their own spot over by the coffeepot along with my coffee mug. They all get washed once a week when I do dishes. It's only my healthy germs so I don't fuss about them.

I bought a grocery cart for my heavy item expeditions. The cart was too low and killed my back the first time I used it. So I returned the cart to the store and went to the wonderful hardware store in the neighborhood and purchased one that was a bit bigger and had a higher handle. That solved the back ache problem. One day I was walking by the bus stop with my loaded grocery cart and one of the men sitting there said, "Wow! That's the Cadillac of grocery carts". And it is a comfortable Caddy.

The grocery cart is perfect for going back and forth to the laundry room. I take hangers along and use the handle to hang up certain garments that I hang on the shower rail to dry. The laundry box in the bottom holds my "delicates" that I hang on a collapsible rack in the bedroom along with other things. My Caddy is multi-purpose.

Another thing that is very handy to have is a folding clothes drying rack. It is perfect for drying your undies and other things that aren't quite dry from the drier or if you don't always use a drier. Have you ever seen sweater drying racks? They are a big square framework with a mesh middle. They have about 6" detachable legs. I keep both of those items handy under the bed and use as necessary. A great convenience.

A bit about decorating. I truly could not get rid of all the collectibles I had accumulated over the years. So I put up shelves 14" or so below the ceiling. The shelves go over the doorways and windows so that is what actually determines the height. They are hung with white "L" shaped metal brackets that are attached to the wall and to the top of the shelf. You put objects in front of the brackets and then they are invisible to the viewer. Good idea, huh? I also added a little grooved molding to the underside of the shelf and a one and a half inch piece of wood to the shelf edge to make it all look more finished. If you want to buy wooden brackets to put underneath to look pretty, do it. I did and they do. Paint every thing the same color as the walls.

A very effective idea that some decorators use is to paint the wall above the shelf a different color. And it does look nice.

When I rented the U-Haul, I brought the painted shelving and all the stuff to be used for display from our house that was finally being sold. It was easy to putty and paint where the shelving had been. And of course, it was much easier for me to take the already assembled shelves with me. Big baskets, either flat or bulky, and serving trays hide the brackets. I arranged the items by color or type of metal. It is more effective and shows off all your treasures so much better. In each group they enhance each other. The blue pitcher draws attention to the blue jar and blue bottle. It's great! Your guests will love it and your ingenuity. And you still have your belongings.

And family pictures. I suggest keeping them in the bedroom. Leave the living room public and don't have your private and personal family all over the place. I placed another little shelf over my twin beds and have pictures of the 14 grandchildren on them. Plus, a shoulder-high book case holds my shoe boxes and there are more grandchildren pictures on that. My parents and ancestors are on the dresser and the walls. It's cozy and warm and makes me feel loved and fortunate.

If you need fresh air at night while you are sleeping, as I do, install a ceiling fan in the bedroom as well as having the window open. Mine runs 24/7 year around. When it's really cold outside and I barely crack open the window at night, I have the illusion of fresh, not stuffy, air. The cool breeze touches my face and I know all is right with the world. There is also a ceiling fan in the kitchen. The bathroom doesn't have a fan or ceiling fixture since the lighting comes from the cabinet lights over the sink. To remedy this, I bought a little battery operated fan that I clip on to some shelving so that it blows towards me on those sticky, hot days when I need ventilation or if the shower has left the room all steamy. You might try a portable electric heater in that windowless bathroom. It tends to eliminate the steam in the colder weather when you don't use the fan. It's amazing how we can adapt to our new environment if we just give ourselves a chance.

Speaking of sleeping in a City. It is amazing how very light it is at night with City lights bright & beautiful outside. Makes for a great view but often is too light for folks who are used to a darker environment at night. Try a sleep mask. Some friends swear by them. Another problem with living in a highrise or any spot in the City is the noise. So try ear plugs. The brand I use is "Quiet Please" and they work beautifully if you follow the directions. Don't give up on a wonderful City living opportunity because there are minor problems. Don't be an old fogey! Try something new and adapt to the surroundings.

Closet space is never what you are used to. Some buildings have had closet experts come in and redesign the units. If that isn't the case, I suggest you divvy up your closet with one space for long things (jumpsuits, etc.) and dresses. And divvy the other space with two high and low racks, one for shirts & blouses and one for pants and vests or whatever. If your closet is such that you can't raise that top rod then buy a dowel the correct length and suspend it from the rod with two chains. You can loop the chains over the top rod & slip the bottom rod through the loops so it hangs evenly. It works. Then hang shorter garments over the new rod such as vests and so forth. Since there isn't room in my bedroom closet, my blazers and jackets and coats all hang together in the hall coat closet. I don't have a coat tree anymore (no space) so I hung one of those wooden expandable racks on the wall for my rain hat, visors, umbrellas and my over-the-shoulder water bottle for the movies. I also have a big old armoire in the hall for sweaters as there isn't room in the bedroom. Actually, there would be but that is where my computer and file cabinet sit. "First things first"

If you are a born-again-decorator like I am, it is difficult to just settle into one color scheme for the rest of your years. It's a depressing thought. My solution is simple. Have a color theme for different seasons of the year. I chose yellow for spring and summer, while red is my choice for fall & winter. I change so many things that my home looks all different and fresh to me. And what fun to unpack a pretty piece that you will enjoy for the next six months. Visa versa when you pack away a favorite piece you know you will be seeing it again when the season is over. I change my bathroom towels & rug, the bedspreads and throw pillows, scatter rugs throughout the house, sliipcovers for two chairs & an ottoman, all the throw pillows in the living room, seat cushions on dining chairs, place mats & napkins, and odds & ends of decorative dishware and accessory pieces. Voila! A New Look!

Be sure to settle on a safe place to keep your most valuable papers. A small fireproof safe that sits in the back of a closet is a good idea. An extra copy of your will and other important papers for the executor of your estate is a necessity. You also might consider an extra key for that person. And be sure to keep that person informed when you go on trips. If you are renting, you might consider putting his/her phone number on the "emergency " line plus the nearest relative. When I go on a trip, I leave a large envelope sitting on my message chair, addressed to my Executor and my children with a note attached saying, "in case of my death, please mail".

Very shortly after you move in, I suggest you find a place to leave messages to yourself or to your housemate. On a chair near the door or your hall table are handy and easily noticed as you are coming or going. But not the refrigerator. It often gets too cluttered with other items. Junk mail envelopes written on with a Magic Marker are perfect for reminders. You don't waste paper and the writing can be huge.

Speaking of messages. When you call a friend and the phone rings 6 – 10 times before the answering machine kicks in, do you get impatient and swear you won't go through that again? Those long waits drive me crazy. Maybe your friends will take the hint if you do the following: Set your answering machine to go on after only 2 rings or the least amount of rings your particular machine allows. Unless you live in a humungus house, you probably can get to the phone before they finish the message. Or if you don't want to talk to that person at that time, you can pass!

I keep my phone ringer in the living room on low and the phone bell in the bedroom is turned off. It's all very nice because if I am asleep the phone doesn't wake me!

If you are fortunate enough to have a deck, patio, balcony, or terrace and you have plants out there, get those little platforms with wheels for your big potted plants. They are so handy and easy to work with. When it's really cold, I push them over next to the warm building. When it rains, I move the ones under cover out into the open. They are so convenient and easy to use. A must for us as we grow older and lose some of our strength. Plant stands on wheel are a necessity if you have a touchy back.

Bird watching is something to consider if you have any out-of-doors area. Get yourself Peterson's Birds of North America or one of his dedicated to a specific area of the country and a pair of bird watching binoculars. Once you discover what kind of birds you have then you can buy the correct seed for particular species. It sounds complicated but it's not. It is such a rewarding hobby that you can share with other birders. Be sure to have a watering trough for your feathered friends. I painted the bottom of a big planter tray a bright blue to attract them. I love to watch the birds enjoy their drinks, especially the Blue Jays who seem to have a unique style of drinking.

Don't forget hummingbirds. Mix ¾ cup of sugar with one quart of water and add a couple drops of red food dye to attract them to your place. You will be amazed at the hummers. You can tell the females from the males by the manner in which they eat. The females perch to eat while the males just hover. Once the hummers get used to their new eating spot, they will come to your window if their food is gone. Sometimes they will even approach a human & just flutter & flutter to get their message across. "Feed me!"

Pets. I love dogs and have always had one or two. It can be difficult to find a place to rent that you like that will accept dogs. There are also the problems involved with exercising them and getting them outside to do their thing. I left our dogs with my husband. Some friends have given their pets to their children and grandchildren. The dogs are still with family and you can at least visit them and not feel you have totally abandoned them and their lifelong love for you.

Cats are something else and are somewhat easier to have in an apartment. Usually you have to make a $200 - $300 deposit, or sometimes pay a fee, to keep a cat or cats.

I cat-sit for friends in my building when they go on vacation. Once the cats are familiar with me, we have a great time. I keep the cat box in the shower (use flushable litter) and put it on the floor when I bathe. It's all very convenient and easy for me. Since I have the bird feeder, I open the blinds from the bottom so the cats can watch. They love it!

I highly recommend renting a storage space in your apartment building, if you need more space. And that also goes for a condo, co-op, and retirement home. They aren't terribly expensive and most places have somewhat adequate closet space but what about the Christmas decorations, out of season clothes, that precious box of old pictures, and so on and so on. That way it's all there and you don't have to make the decision to part with those valuables yet. I happen to believe that we shouldn't "throw the baby out with the bath water". It's all too many decisions. Wait a while. Wait a few years. You have time.

"A place for everything and everything in its place"

BUDGETING

"A penny saved is a penny earned"

There are so many choices that we must make if we are on any kind of a budget. It seems to me it all comes down to a question of what is the most important. And often the choices are over such trivial, silly things like I shouldn't spend twice as much for those super delicious home-grown ripen-on-the-vine tomatoes or I can drink cheaper Vodka than Stoly's. And sometimes, it's a question of life style such as if I want to travel I can't afford this apartment or why do I need a car?

I read a book that my long ago mentor, Kathleen, recommended called *The Choice is Always Ours*, that has empowered me over the years. I never finished the whole book but I learned to believe in the title. We all have choices all the time. Some are major and most are minor. I think one of the big problems that couples have is making decisions. It seems that often one mate will say, "oh, it doesn't matter. You decide." Then when it does matter and something goes wrong, the oh-so-innocent non-participant will say, "Hey, you got us into this, now what are you going to do?" or "You picked it out". Is that a classic case of passive aggressive behavior, or what? Don't get into that over money or anything else if you can possibly help it. I don't care to discuss psychology in this book just some hints from the costly trip here. But remember the choice is (almost) always ours.

Some of this budget stuff sounds so petty and insignificant. But the cents and then dollars all add up. It is a way of life that some of us have to abide by. So be tolerant and maybe you'll even learn something.

When I first moved here I decided to keep track of every cent that I spent. I got a small spiral notebook and jot down everything I spend during the month: movie 5-, groceries 36-, dry cleaning 8-, wine 6-, lunch 7-, etc. At the end of each month I take the notebook & my checkbook and list every amount under its proper heading: groceries, entertainment, lodging, subscriptions, charity, medical, hair, transportation, etc. The categories are determined by your life style. Then I total the month to see what I have spent. At the end of the year I total each category and learn what I really did. It's an excellent way to find out where your money goes. Plus if you do it right, your tax deductions are already totaled for the year.

Those home grown ripened-on-the-vine tomatoes to me are almost as good as chocolate ice cream. They give me so much pleasure. I ooh and aah every time I slice one and eat them with my dinner or put one slice on a grilled kielbasa sandwich. To me the other tomatoes just don't count. The problem is they cost so much. How do I rationalize their expense? Often I don't because I like them so-o-o much. In the summer I do grow my own in a big pot in a sunny spot on the terrace. But that's only the summer. It's the rest of the year that is expensive. Am I satisfying a whim? I don't know & I don't care. If I didn't buy those I wouldn't eat any tomatoes, so I make the choice each week to splurge and have learned to only eat a half of a tomato at a time rather than a whole one. They last twice as long. "Tomorrow is another day!"

One of my favorite drinks is Stoly on the rocks. But I decided that I could drink good Vodka for half the money and I didn't need to splurge on Stoly's. The lady at the liquor store suggested Burnett's. Once I added an olive and 2 or 3 drops of lemon juice, I couldn't tell the difference! (Tomatoes are more important). When I drink Smooth Move Tea, a natural laxative, I switch to Old-Fashions and fill up the glass with Tea. In fact I drink it from a tumbler rather than a cocktail glass. And I buy the least expensive bourbon there is, because with bitters, sugar, and the tea I can't taste any of it. Good deal. The dental hygienist suggested drinking the old fashioned with a straw because the tea and bitters tends to stain the teeth. Thought I would pass that on, too.

I'm so grateful that I don't smoke any more. Often street people ask for spare change and if he/she is smoking I always say, "If you didn't smoke, you would have money for food".

It may not do any good but it makes me feel better. Smoking is too expensive besides all the other baggage smoking involves.

My one-bedroom apartment is really a nice one in my opinion. It's in a 50-year-old building. There is a small bedroom and hardly any closet space and a small kitchen but it has a workable size living room, a view, and a couple other nice amenities. I lucked out and just fell into this by living in the building and keeping my eyes and ears open to know when it was vacated. Keep that in mind when you're looking at apartments. If you like the location then move in to what is available and tell the rental agent to keep you posted on other units as they become available. Being a rental agent myself, I know how busy they are so make a friendly pest of yourself and check with the front desk fairly often. It works! My friend, Pam, did that also to get a unit with a balcony and eventually got it. She didn't even unpack for three months. Patience is a virtue. Location. Location. Location. Conrad Hilton's famous words.

For three years I traveled and did all sorts of things that I really enjoyed, like expensive restaurants, expensive seats at the opera and symphony, Elderhostel trips hither and yon. All delightful, educational and so very enjoyable. But after living here a while and going over my money situation and my inherited long-living-future-gene, I decided I needed to make a few changes. So I have.

First I cut back on the above. I still go to the opera & symphony & plays once in a while but we sit in the cheap seats in the upper reaches with our binoculars. Acoustics are great and we hear everything. Some dress rehearsals are open to the public and sometimes I attend those. The ballet practices in a big tent in the park in the summer with rows of seats for comfort. And that is always fun. Take your lunch and enjoy the entertainment.

I very seldom eat out and find I don't miss it at all. I shop at Costco once or twice a year and fill up the freezer. It's amazing how long frozen food lasts when you are only cooking for one. I learned an important lesson within a month after arriving. I had never cooked for just one person so I wasted a lot of fresh produce because I didn't plan very well and it would spoil before I got to it. Really caught me unaware. Not anymore. I just walk the four blocks to the store more often or stop on my way home from OASIS. When I invite people up for a drink at the end of the day, I say, "bring your own pleasure". And visa versa. I reciprocate. No one minds and we aren't guzzling each other's booze. Many of us are watching our pennies and we all respect that.

One of the things special about our building, and some others I have been in, is they have a Community Room where you can recycle your magazine subscriptions and any books you want to get rid of. A great place to pick up something you wish to read. Something a friend and I did was he gave his magazines to me when he was through and I gave him mine. Now I only subscribe to Newsweek and the Oregonian is delivered daily. Then in time we take the magazines to the Community Room for other tenants to enjoy.

Often some of the restaurants in town have a special Senior rate at certain hours. Most of the bars in town have a special Cocktail Hour rate, if you want to have a treat. The movies give us a break, too. I am a member of the Goodwill and shop on Thursdays as that is the day we Seniors get an additional discount. It costs nothing to join. I love the Goodwill for picking up T-shirts or sweatshirts for the grandkids. Be sure to check out jeans and khakis, too. The name brands are a must for teens and what bargains there are. Safeway has a discount card and it is amazing the savings on some items. Warning: Don't buy it just because it is on sale. Only buy what you will use. Otherwise, it's "Penny wise and pound foolish".

Some of you are probably at the same stage in your life that I am. I certainly don't need any new furniture or "stuff". What I spend my money on are necessities: Housing, food, medical and some entertainment including TV and the telephone.

Expensive food is first to go and unnecessary entertainment is next. And I try to stay healthy so I don't have medical bills, other than that damn HMO payment. If I need an article of clothing I check around and depending what it is, I may pick it up at a used clothing or second-hand store. There is good stuff out there and treasures to find.

When planning retirement, something to really think about is: What am I going to need or what is going to wear-out when I am retired? I'm talking about linens and other household goods. Buy them before you retire while you are more flexible with your expenditures. Another thing to consider: What is going to bother me in the future when I have less? If it involves money, think very carefully about the decisions you are making for retirement before you make them permanent.

An option to consider if you are staying in your same house in your same community is reverse mortgages. So far everything I have heard is positive. It is something to investigate. As I have vehemently proclaimed, I am not an expert so I can only pass on ideas for you to investigate.

What really helps me is my job. I work as a rental agent for a good-sized investment company as a "floater" in their different apartment buildings when someone is ill or on vacation. I mostly work on week-ends because I am so involved at OASIS with learning and teaching. Years ago before and during the time I was back in school, I worked part-time for Eichler Homes in Santa Clara as a sales person showing co-ops. A good place to learn. Plus my other job experiences over the years have me well qualified as a people person and that is the kind of work I do. I first worked for ten months on week-ends in the building

I live in. Then I got burned out and now I'm not locked into a strict routine and can say No when I feel it necessary

I have been amazed at the part-time jobs that are available out there. Anti-age discrimination is our friend. For instance, Wayne in California, is a greeter for a big auto dealer in his area. Jack has continued in insurance sales but has scaled back a bit. John does part-time consulting in the medical field. Teri has continued her wonderfully, fulfilling career in real estate sales. Bill, Eunice, and Boyd prepare taxes for H&R Block during the tax season. This is a wonderful job for only four months a year. A special part of it for Seniors is that clients trust you just because you are old and therefore experienced. Quite an advantage over the younger preparers.

For all sorts or opportunities, check out the want ads and ask your friends. Call businesses that are similar to what you did before. Age and experience are on your side. Probably no one can afford to pay you what you're worth, but so what. If you want a little job to help you along and will take less, it's out there and you'll find it.

What I have learned this past year is that I get tired and that I need two days off in a row. One to catch up and one to relax. Age is catching up with me and I have to adjust accordingly. Remember that and don't take on too much. Some of us never slow down and manage beautifully and some of us learn as we go. So learn this: "Just say No." There are times when that is extremely difficult if you need the money or if the activity is going to be tons of fun. If you must do it, then give up something else 'cause you can't do anything if you're flat on your back in the hospital!

SETTLING IN

"Give in on the little things, but never give in on the big things"

Do you know the difference?

GETTING INVOLVED

"Do unto others as you would have them do unto you"

I returned to Portland July first and the furniture van arrived within a day or two. After the furniture was unpacked and placed as planned, my belongings unpacked and the refrigerator supplied, it was time to do something. I wasn't sure what but Tracy didn't leave me much time to wonder. She told me she had been taking T'ai Chi and to come with her to a class.

We took the bus to the major department store in town, Meier & Frank, and went up in the elevator to the 10th floor to an area that had a big sign saying, Welcome to OASIS. I was introduced to the instructor and we proceeded to do T'ai Ch Chih. I loved it. So much in fact that I took it for three years. I have a video now and do it when I feel the need. The new classes teach a different form of T'ai Chi that I don't care as much for, so I haven't taken the classes lately. Others do and love it. I'm probably missing out by not giving it a thorough try but I have my video and don't need the group as much nor do I have the time that I did those first few years.

What is this OASIS? Older Adult Service & Information System is what the original letters meant. It is now more a national education program and enrichment program for adults over 50. It used to be 55. I will copy from its catalog so you'll know. There are centers in AZ, CA, CO, D.C., IL, IN, MD, MO, NM, NY, OH, OK, OR, PA, & TX. Members must be over 50 years. Membership is free. "OASIS is the largest, most comprehensive educational and volunteer service program for mature adults in the U.S. It provides a broad range of opportunities for more than 360,000 members to explore new ideas and share their experiences. The mission of OASIS is to enrich the lives of mature adults." Maybe knowing that OASIS is in a part of the country where you live or where you are considering moving will help you to make a decision.

If you have a department store in your area owned by the May Company, you are really in luck. They are one of the main sponsors of OASIS and can probably give you information. Legacy Health System along with Blue Cross are co-sponsors in Portland. Also, Blue Shield is the tutor program sponsor for K – 3 grades. Maybe you could be instrumental in starting an OASIS in your area. Talk about doing your community a service! What a feeling of pride that could be.

If you are an "interested-in-learning" person, OASIS is for you. Their catalog comes out 3 times a year and lists the programs (classes) it is offering to meet the diverse interests and needs of its members, including performing arts; travel & travelogues; health; exercise; arts, music & humanities; computers & technology; financial & legal; personal, practical & fun information; plus exciting volunteer opportunities to assist OASIS and the community. The national phone number in St. Louis to call for information regarding locations of OASIS: 314 862 - 2933. E-mail: WWW.OASISNET.ORG

Well, I was hooked and where do I sign up? Many of the classes are free and any fees are truly minimal. I think the most expensive I have seen is $20. Many are about $3.00. The health classes are all free. The organization is very aware of limited funds for many of its members. Some classes are a one shot thing for one to two hours with a potty break in the middle. Others meet once a week for anywhere from two to ten weeks. The people are there because they want to be and because the class is something that interests them.

There are three "semesters", Winter-Spring, Summer, & Fall. Some terms I find that I have signed up for 3 or 4 classes a week and sometimes 2 in one day. I love it. It keeps me learning and it's a wonderful place to meet people. A sampling of classes: book review groups, movie review groups, discussion groups talking about the news, there are renowned guest lecturers, there are classes in music history & appreciation, there are cooking classes, there are exercise groups, walking groups, basket weaving, calligraphy, there are travel groups and all kinds of computer courses. There is a smattering of everything. I took several writing classes the first three years and if you are ever here you are welcome to enroll in the one I now teach twice a year, or just sit in on a class or two. (limited to 12 students)

The OASIS in Portland has a lending library that is open during OASIS hours and is run totally by volunteers. The person in charge of the library is a retired librarian, which is a good deal for all of us, and is especially rewarding to Helen. On Thursdays there is a retired male nurse on duty for a couple of hours to take the blood pressure of anyone who so desires. I take advantage of this whenever I am at OASIS on a Thursday. It's smart to be aware.

In practically any town you are going to find multiple opportunities to meet people. I truly believe that if you do the things you enjoy, you will meet others doing the same. A wonderful way to make new friends. There are churches, adult education, volunteer groups, mentor groups, hospitals, libraries, museums. Think about tutoring. And sports. If you play golf or tennis or racquetball or bowl or play bridge or mah jong or various other games, there are groups and clubs everywhere. Just start. Have you always wanted to have professional lessons in water color or any other art skill? How 'bout learning to play the piano at long last? Now is the perfect time. Try calling the Chamber of Commerce or just simply ask your neighbors or any of the old timers. Do it!

From the survey I found that over 70% of Seniors do volunteer work. Some are involved in many organizations as board members while others do all kinds of menial work. The reasoning was totally the same: "I enjoy it. It is satisfying. I will continue." Volunteering has many faces and one of those is stuffing envelopes. A large plus for this menial task is the minimum of concentration needed which gives one the perfect opportunity to chat with your fellow volunteers. Who knows you may meet your new best friend! Many have been doing it for several years and have no intention of quitting until they can't do it anymore.

Sometimes it seems that volunteer work is all stuffing envelopes and adding sticker address labels to those same envelopes. That's OK. It is still valuable and useful work for the organization you are helping. Often the best part is chatting with and getting to know the people with whom you are sharing this boring job. "Remember when we stuffed that endless supply of envelopes, etc. etc.?" Or if there is only one of you doing this tedious job, ask for a helper. Explain how the job will go faster and you will be more inclined to volunteer again if you aren't bored to death first. Do help. It's worth it.

An interesting and fun activity to consider is Little Theatre or whatever the group is called in your community. My friend, Jeri in Florida, acts, directs, sells tickets, is a stage hand or whatever is needed at the time. OASIS has a production group also and they put on a simple play at the end of each semester. We all seem to love theatre and if you have any talent or experience or just love participating, this could be just the ticket for you. Try it!

In my other life I was very active in Friends of the Library so here I decided to do something different and volunteer at the Art Museum. I have been doing half a day once or twice a month for almost five years now. I have learned so much when special traveling exhibits are in town and, of course, met many new people. My volunteer time is limited because I take all those classes and believe it or not, I get tired! But it's a wonderful tiredness. It's all out there if you just dig in and do it!

In an apartment complex or condos or any group of homes there is usually a neighborhood bulletin board. If not, you make one and put it someplace. The bulletin board is a great place to put notices to start different groups, bridge, mah jong, bowling, baseball, etc. Something else you might consider is suggesting they get a program or recreation director, either paid or volunteer. You might be just the one for the job. Notices of items for sale or meetings coming up, or lost animals can be posted there.

You might think about starting an In The News group. Meet once a week and everyone brings a newspaper or magazine clipping that interests him or her. The members read pertinent parts of it aloud and then everyone discusses it. You might do local & U.S. news every week except the first meeting of each month could be designated for foreign news. It's wonderful to hear different opinions from others besides your mate and close friends, if you even discuss such things with them. We have found in our group that religion and politics are no-no's. As you can imagine, these topics can become too personal and cause problems we don't need. You will need a group leader or it can lead to chaos as the topics get more interesting. It might take a while but it will catch on.

Tutoring young children to read better or helping older kids get a better grip on their studies has got to be one of the most rewarding volunteer jobs a person can do. The hours necessary are different in each community but find out about this for the greatest satisfaction you can imagine. The enormous pleasure both you and the child will feel in raising his/her grades from D's & F's to an A, B, or C is unbelievable. You are laying the groundwork for a potential failure in life to become an educated success. These kids never forget who helped them either. You will have a young friend for life.

It's been my experience that lending books to many Seniors is the same as giving them away. They do not intentionally keep them. They simply forget. So to try to insure that your belongings are returned to you: 1) put your name in all your books before letting them out of your sight and 2) keep a list of the books and the people to whom you lend them. I have lost at least two of my best books (Care of the Back and The Choice

Is Always Ours) because I didn't write them down. The person I think I lent them to claims not to have them. If I had a list we would both know. Start this process earlier than I did. And that's a suggestion from a dim-witted ex-librarian whose books are missing.

Before I end this chapter, I must mention computers again. As you know they are everywhere. If you are one of the unfortunate seniors who never got involved for some reason or other, put all that behind you and jump in feet first. Believe me, you are not the only one who doesn't know squat about computers. Join a beginner's class. Ask at the library, adult education, night school, Kinko's, or other stores that have computer usage open to the public. There is a vast world out there to enjoy if you will just let yourself. Especially, if you are a shut-in there is more to life than the television. There are people who make their living helping people solve computer problems in their homes for a relatively modest fee. Diana is my mentor who either answers my problems via e-mail or we make an appointment. And often teachers give seniors a reduced rate. There are advantages to being a senior. Honest.

And e-mail. I turn on my computer first thing in the morning even before I turn on the coffee. By the time I am dressed my e-mail is up and I can begin my morning with a message. I joined Classmates to help me connect with my high school graduating class and it's wonderful. Then I joined "A joke a day" and get these funny jokes and one-liners each morning. It's something I have found that starts the day off with a smile. But of course, the best thing about e-mail is getting a message from one of the grandchildren, or one of your kids, or from a friend. It is such a fast and easy way to communicate that if you don't use your computer for anything else, use it for e-mail! You all know how wonderful and helpful computers are but for you that are reluctant: Get with it - Join the 21st century.

And wives! Is your husband just sitting around for one reason or another and just doesn't seem to know what to do with himself since he retired? This could be for the retired working wife as well. Mostly I have heard this complaint from the wives though. Get him/her a computer and private lessons until he/she is comfortable learning in public. Tracy's husband spends the day on his computer and communicates with people in other countries, practices his Spanish and even has had an article published in Peru. Think how wonderful that is for him. He's 84 and not in the best of health. It's a godsend for him and oh my! how Tracy loves being by herself sometimes when he is home. Some women seem to need that time for themselves like it was before he retired. This solves the problem and is perfect for both.

MAKING NEW FRIENDS

"You catch more flies with honey than you do with vinegar"

When I moved into this 190-unit apartment building, I didn't know a single person. I was lucky it just happened that two other senior women moved in that same week. We were constantly running into each other as we learned our way around and solved various problems that always arise in a new place. Doris had to move to a nursing home last year but Jeanette and I are still here and we are always there for each other. We don't do a lot of the same things in our lives but when our paths cross, it is a warm welcome for us both.

I became very good friends with two different neighbors I had. I lived next door to Pat for a year and Kathy a little longer than that. We each still live here and have our own lives but we make it a point to do something together even if only talking on the phone or having a cup of coffee occasionally just to keep up and let the other one know we care. Pat often comes over on Sunday nights and watches HBO with me. What are friends for?

I do want to mention the type of people I have found that live in big apartment buildings. It's an eclectic potpourri! That's how I describe us. We have all ages, colors, religions, and life styles. It's delightful. If you take the time you can learn and enjoy so much. Just a friendly Hi in the elevator and even a dumb comment about the weather can be an icebreaker. Leave those small-town prejudices behind you. You might hear different languages being spoken. Forget the attitude of: If they live here, why don't they speak our language. That isn't your concern. Just be nice and welcome to the 21st century.

Living in any new community is a wonderful way to grow and expand your horizons. Often in retirement living environments we sit at the same table with the same people at each meal. May I suggest that you choose one meal and every day at that time sit at a different table to meet and enjoy the other tenants. It's a wonderful opportunity to learn and to display your love of the world and its inhabitants. And I mean people of a different color, religion, life style and whatever else there is. That may sound silly and "pie in the sky" but it's true. Open the blinders and be part of what's out there.

My friends in the building range in age from 20's to people in their 80's. It is delightful and each is coming from his/her own place in the world and has ideas of all sorts. The younger ones seem receptive to me and are always invited to my Open Houses. Heather is in her 20's and I baby-sit her two cats when she travels. I love having them run to greet me when I open the door and sit on my lap for a purr session! And Heather is content knowing her pets are well taken care of in her absence. I love animals and have found pet sitting to be very rewarding without having the constant responsibility. At one point Heather felt guilty because Tua & Oliver needed care for three weeks. I agreed to take $5.00 a day for those three weeks. It freed her from guilt and was a nice bon bon for me. I will be doing the same for my darling, young friend Hillary when she goes to Greece.

At Oasis I found a home away from home. The volunteer helpers are so thoughtful and kind. I have met several women and men taking the same classes that I do there, that I really enjoy. On occasion we have done things socially and it's terrific. Just like you have known them forever. Once that connection is started, give it a chance. Make it possible for a friendship to develop. Suggest lunch or a cup of coffee or a cocktail, or whatever, but do something. It's so easy to suggest going to a movie to fellow students from the Brown Bag Movie Review group. Give these opportunities a boost. Some people are so shy & cautious. You be the brave one and you'll be amazed at the benefits.

I met Pam at Oasis and we have had great fun together. We go to plays, concerts, and movies and have meals with each other once in a while. She has a cabin in the woods at a lake in Washington and we go up there and solve the problems of the world. If one of us has a particular thorn, we role-play. It's a terrific way to see the other side and hopefully solve what is bothering one of us. She always has projects to complete and I have a book to read or I just sit and hear the silence while I enjoy the view. And sometimes I even help with the project. She has health problems but never complains. Quite a gal!

I continue to feel that for women, there is nothing better in the world than a girl friend.

One you can talk to, who accepts you mostly for who you are, whom you trust and who trusts you, and is honest, kind and with a sense of humor. Men have these same wants, and especially need to be encouraged when retired to keep up those relationships and to make new friends, if in a new and different community. What else is there?

One of the things I have done to keep in touch with my friends that don't live in town is to send a Christmas letter in December and a summer letter in June. They know I am thinking of them and usually I get a reply in July. Isn't it great to open that little locked mailbox to discover a letter from a dear friend or a fond relative? It's easy to do with a computer. Print it and go get copies made. Typewriters work, too. I made a checklist chart when I started that two-letters-a-year idea. I make a line in dated column by the name of people I mail to, and then when they reply, I cross it and make an X. Some people are letter writers and some aren't. It doesn't matter, keep in touch anyway. We all love to receive mail.

I love receiving letters all year long and Christmas cards when 'tis the season. And I especially love receiving pictures of my friends. But I am always perplexed when people send me pictures of their grandchildren. It's fun to see how their kids turned out (if I knew them back when) but seeing the unknown grandkids doesn't do much for me. And I was amazed at how many of my fellow Seniors felt the same way. Send yourself, not a substitute!

Not too long ago I had a sad experience. Dorothy's son, Mike, called me from California to tell me the sad news that his Mom had died. The only way he knew my address for sure was from my letter to her that arrived not too long after her death. I wasn't part of the funeral but was able to share some memories on the phone with Mike. Keep in touch.

My first Christmas here was a fiasco because of the weather and my driving to Walla Walla. I decided then and there that

that wasn't going to happen again. So the following Holiday and Thanksgiving I got together with the older "rootless" people I liked here. That means those particular friends of any age who don't have family near by and are alone for the holidays. Not anymore. We have dinner here and I do the turkey, dressing, gravy and mashed potatoes. They sign up and bring the vegetables (peas), cranberry sauces (jellied and whole), pumpkin pie and whipped cream, mincemeat pie, and whatever else we need in the dish it is to be served in. And everyone brings one bottle of white wine. We drink it before and during and occasionally after. Just depends. There have been anywhere from 6 - 10 people here. I also usually ask everyone to bring an empty plate so I can send him or her home with leftovers. When I make the turkey soup from the bones 2 or 3 of them return for that treat. The total occasion is a wonderful happy time for us all.

Time to share my turkey recipe with you. It's from The Chronicle at least 45 years ago.

This will do a 12 to 22 lb. bird. Clean it out and then stuff it. Tie it up. I save my bacon drippings and rub that cold bacon fat all over the turkey. Place in a paper grocery bag & tie the end. Put in a roasting pan & place in a COLD oven. Bake 1 hour at 500', then 1 hour at 400', and 1 hour at 300'. And that's it! No basting, just set the timer to remind you when each hour is up. Take turkey out of roasting pan, put on the carving platter and remove the hot greasy paper. Be careful. While the turkey is settling, you make the gravy. The drippings have hardly any grease or fat because the paper bag has absorbed it all. The juice in the bottom of the roasting pan is just that – Juice! The gravy is wonderful! Happy Holiday!

Another festivity I have is an Open House on December 21st and June 21st. One for summer and one for the winter holiday. Same day every year and I don't have to remember or figure out the best date. You can pick any date you want once or twice a year. It becomes a tradition and everyone looks forward to it. I invite about 50 people and usually 20-30 show up. On the first invitation I called it an "Open House that flows into the hall". I also invite every one on my floor so they can't complain about the noise and it's a good way to meet your neighbors. If you live in a house, invite the whole block along with your other friends. The hours for my party are from 5:30 to 7:30. I just slide the hand written invitations under the doors and don't ask for an RSVP. Some people have such good manners that they reply anyway but it really doesn't matter. Sometimes every one leaves on time but once in a while there are hangers-on that stick around. And that's great. We just drink more punch. Or order a pizza. For munchies, I serve cold veggies and some green grapes with chunks of Monterey Jack cheese and maybe some crackers or nuts. It ain't fancy. It's simple and so easy. We all have fun!

Champagne Punch
1 big bottle of cheap white wine, chilled. I prefer something dry, like Chardonnay
1 big bottle of cheap champagne, chilled.
1 or 2 big bottles (1 qt. ea.) grapefruit SODA, chilled

And that's it. Whole strawberries can be added. I don't. It just adds complications. The amount of soda determines the strength of the punch. 2 qts. of the soda makes approximately 18 to 20 servings. So 1 qt. of soda is probably 12-15 servings.

Use the amount of soda that satisfies your taste and desired strength.

To make the ice, I fill a few Tupperware containers with water and put them in the freezer. They are easy to handle and the ice blocks come out readily by running water over the bottoms. Plus you aren't diluting the punch as quickly as you do with dinky ice cubes.

I usually have enough ingredients on hand to make 3 or 4 punch bowls full. Any left over I put in a liter and use it during the week. Unopened bottles get put away for next time.

It's easy to make friends if you are pleasant, happy and friendly. Some people get in our elevator or are in classes and never say a word. They keep their heads down and are very quiet. And that's OK if it works for them. If that doesn't suit you, get out and join some groups, start smiling and you'll be amazed at the eventual results! I think almost every community has a Senior Center. Just ask. Good luck.

The survey had a section on Social Life and they were asked to choose the category that best described their social life. 1)Busy 2)Perfect 3) So-So 4) Dull were the choices.

Some chose not to answer so I don't have a total of 100% but this is what I got. Dull got one response. And the other three were between 25% and 30%. That should be encouraging to you newcomers to the Senior world.

Some words of caution. It's very easy to get caught up in the ritual of having cocktails with friends, either out or at home. My experience has been that often one drink isn't enough, a second is being suggested and sometimes even a third. Don't fall into that trap. It's hard enough to stay healthy and trim without adding all the calories that alcohol has plus what it can do to your personality. What 3 or 4 or 5 nightly drinks can do to you and your life is sad. So be careful with those well-meaning friends. You are all walking a fine line in many ways if you over indulge. You can always choose to stay home and have your cocktail with Larry King, the evening news or a rousing game of pinochle, cribbage, or solitaire on the computer. It does work.

Kathleen's husband left her for another woman when they were in their mid 60's. She was devastated and totally lost her self-confidence, her self-esteem and that feeling of lovely femininity that women usually have. She was engaged in all sorts of civic causes and groups in her town, plus being an active church member serving on various committees. She continued with her responsibilities and activities all the while being grateful that she had the diversion and the rewards of her obligations. It didn't take a mate's place but it helped through some lean and empty months.

It was through a human rights committee that she met Steve who was 25 years younger than her 65 years. As it sometimes happens, their meeting really struck a needful chord in both of them. They became fast and dear friends and formed a friendship that continues to this day. It is not a sexual relationship. He still dates others but continues to treat Kathleen to dinners, movies, plays and sometimes even a hike whenever they can arrange a time. Steve has been such a comfort in Kathleen's life and she in his. They have learned that each can trust and rely on the other. Fifteen years later, they both know how very fortunate each one is to have found such a good and true friend.

"If you can't say something nice about a person, don't say anything at all"

DATING DO'S & DON'TS

Asking a person out for the first time in many years takes a bit of skill I have been told. Personally, I think it's quite simple. Be honest. Be specific. Be flexible. Don't be so shy that you miss out. If you meet someone you want to know, go for it. These suggestions may apply for a man or a woman.

Being specific –
   Person #1 –Will you have dinner with me Tuesday?
   Person #2 - Yes, that sounds very nice.

The details can be ironed out as the conversation progresses or with a phone call.

Be sure to tell Person #2 where you are going so he/she knows what to wear.

Being flexible –
   Person #1 – Would you have dinner with me on Tuesday?
   Person #2 – That sounds so nice but I have plans. How about Wednesday?
   Person #1 - That would be just fine. I will call you that morning. What's your number?

Or

Person #1 – Would you have dinner with me on Tuesday?

Person #2 – That sounds so nice, but I have plans.

Person #1 – Oh, that's too bad. How about Wednesday?

Person #2 – Wednesday is perfect. Thank you.

Person #1 – I will call you Tuesday to finalize our plans. What is your phone number?

Doesn't all that make good sense? It's polite & communicative.

What do you think of these obnoxious, nothing questions?

Person #1 – What are you doing tomorrow?

Person #1 – How does your week look?

Person #1 - What are you doing today?

What would you answer? "Call me. I have to look at my calendar." or "Did you have something in mind?" or "Why are you asking?" There are other options. I personally prefer not to get Person #1 started on that ambiguous, non-specific, probing-into-your-personal-life track and in a bad habit if the relationship grows, so how about, "It's none of your business" for an answer, because it isn't (said in a nice way, of course).

This is my favorite. If Person #1 responds to "Why are you asking" with "I wanted to ask you out", please reply, "Then do it". If you want to share your calendar, then that is your prerogative but believe me, it will become a bad and annoying habit that you have condoned.

Person #1 could also say to you, "I'm going to the concert on Tuesday, would you like to come?

I find that such an informative and pleasant question. Person #1 got it right, at last!

Most of us have been married or in a relationship for years and years and over that long period of time we sometimes lose the skills of communication in the beginning of a new relationship. I have a friend who calls those long time relationship decision-making-processes a "committee meeting". Whatever it is called, when you are alone, it ain't that way anymore. There is no committee.

This person is not already your mate and cannot read your mind. He/she doesn't want to and won't. Being turned down is not the end of the earth. Tell the person what you have in mind. Don't be so damn vague. Keep at it. Don't give up. You can do it. Good luck!

KISSING

That doesn't sound like a big deal. You have been kissing since you were a kid and you certainly know how to do it. Forgive me, but it has probably been a while, maybe even a very long time since you kissed a new person in your life. Now that you have finally asked this new person out, or agreed to go out, then what? OK, here goes. Lunch, dinner, drinks, a movie, whatever the occasion, eventually the time has come to end the date

For her: Sometimes it is easier to say Good-Night in the car, thank him for a lovely evening, give him a quick kiss on the cheek (only if you are so inclined), open the car door yourself and walk to the front door. Turn around, wave and go into the house or your building, condo or apartment. Be sure you wave and give everyone a last look and a nice feeling.

Or when he walks you to the door, have your keys ready, do the same thing and go inside. I suggest not asking him to come inside on this first date. Give both of you time to cherish the evening and to learn more about each other. Sometimes a peck on the cheek is OK, but I think it's better to skip it on the first date. Then he doesn't know whether to return the kiss, go on to bigger things, or what. Much easier not to get involved on the doorstep so quickly.

For him: Don't rush the kissing thing. It makes women edgy and wonder about your intentions. So, open the car door for her and walk her to the door, look at her nicely, thank her for a lovely evening, say good-night, walk to the car, and drive away.

If she kisses you on the cheek, nod appreciatively, say, "that was nice. Thank you. I had a lovely evening, I'll call you", and go to the car, turn around, wave, and leave! Good memories.

What you have both done is share a special beginning and left each of you to want more!

And do not terrify the other person by coming on too strong. As you have more dates, spend more time together, get to know one another better, kissing will definitely become more a part of your lives. Good luck! Of course, if the evening was a total flop. Thank the person for the nice meal, movie, whatever and just say good-night. Don't mention calling again.

Of course, there are always exceptions and sometimes the whole date has been so fabulous and you both seem so well matched that you can't help yourselves. That does happen and it's great! I just don't want either of you to have regrets in the morning and that won't happen if you show restraint for a little while. More good luck!!

When the time comes for more subtle, suggestive, hungry kisses, please, keep your tongue in your own mouth. Sexy kisses are with the lips slightly parted, and maybe a small nibble, with more quiet kisses without smacking out loud but closing and opening the lips a bit slowly and gently throughout. If you don't know how to do this, practice on the back of your hand. You'll know when you have it right. These long slow suggestive, romantic, sexy kisses are the best! Save that damn tongue for when you have progressed to taking off your clothes. It totally ruins the mood if done prematurely.

The thing about kissing someone new for the first time is so special and you don't want to scare anyone away. The goal is to show that you know what is going on but that you are new at this also, and want to, need to, take it slow. It's worth it and will set a lovely comfortable stage for a loving, demonstrative romance as you know each other better if that is what you want.

However, do not forget that with kissing like this you both should be aware of where this will end. You may not know when but you both know why. So, please if you have any doubts about full-fledged sex, now is the time to bring it out into the open. It's not fair, polite, or nice to be led on and on and not come to a satisfactory conclusion for both of you. (Men: If you want her, then your goal should be to gently get her to want you)

Some where in the dating routine there comes a time to discuss any worries either of you might have about the relationship and about sex itself. Oral sex, manual stimulation, STD (sexually transmitted disease), Viagara (YES!), blood tests, etc. are some of the topics to be discussed. Both of you must participate in this discussion, so be prepared when the subjects come up naturally.

For females: I must remind you to be extra cautious with strangers that you meet out of nowhere and have no one to vouch for their sterling character.. If you live in an apartment building you can meet him in the lobby and come and go from there. If you live in a house you might arrange to drive your own vehicle and rendezvous with him at the appointed destination. Or if he insists on picking you up (macho) then hop out of the car by yourself as I mentioned before. Really, be careful and don't ask someone into your place until you are truly certain he is OK! Most guys are really nice people but one never knows.

For males: The same advice applies to you. One never knows and you don't want to be accused of something like assault or rape or robbery and end up in court or settling a sum of money on a stranger. So, stay zipped up until you know more about her. There are nasty people out there looking for opportunities and one never knows for sure. Most women are wonderful, just be cautious anyway.

Awhile back I was with a neutral male friend having a drink in the bar of a restaurant and met a guy named Jim. After chatting and buying us both drinks and finding out that my date was not my boy friend, he asked for my phone number and surprising to me, I gave it to him. What I didn't tell Jim was that I have only given out my phone number to a stranger in a bar twice before in my life and I ended up marrying both of them twenty years apart! My point is when you meet someone new, that you are attracted to and he/she responds in kind, do go that extra mile to become friends and find out if there is something there. But, don't let him into your living quarters until you know him better

Jim did call me and we had lunch a few times and drinks once in a while. What I discovered early on was that drinking was what Jim liked. Hell, we met in a bar! So the budding relationship never blossomed as that was not the kind of life or total entertainment I was interested in. We still hook up for a drink now and then, but that's it. And he still hasn't seen my abode!

My philosophy about meeting new people is "Do what you enjoy doing and you will meet other people doing the same". It's not always easy to figure out what you enjoy, but you can. Hike, swim, ski, sail, sing, dance, read, paint, ride horseback, tennis, little theatre, etc to name a few!

ODDS 'N ENDS TIDBITS LEFTOVERS MISCELLANEOUS WANTS AND NEEDS

Often when older men talk about women, they talk about what females want from men and why they go out with them. They think that all (most) older women want someone to take them to the grocery store, cleaners, shopping, etc. Just someone to drive them around. Men claim that women won't go anywhere on their own and are looking for an escort to pay the bill.. They also think that older women aren't interested in sex anymore.

And what do women think that all (most) older men want? They think they want someone to do the laundry, cook their meals, clean up their home, etc.. They think that men are couch potatoes, non-adventurous, unable to think for themselves or take responsibility for their decisions. And some women think older men like to talk about sex but are afraid to actually do it anymore unless it is with a young chickie.

Isn't it sad the perceptions that these Seniors are stuck with? The problem, it seems to me is, don't try to argue or prove a point. The solution is to be yourself and to be honest in your expressions about feelings, needs, and desires.

Sometimes it is nice just to have a good friend and companion of the opposite sex. After a couple of dates, you'll know whether the relationship has possibilities or if it will never progress beyond a nice friendship. Hey, that's OK. The opposite sex can give you a different viewpoint on many of the things you may be struggling with or are thinking about in another person. Hang on to those friendships.

However, if the dating goes on down that more romantic path then by all means and most of all, BE YOURSELF and BE HONEST !! And insist that your prospective partner do the same, otherwise you both will be sorry down the road. And it can be a rocky road just because you're older and aren't the same old spry and agile person you used to be. And the responsibility one faces if the other becomes ill or incapacitated can be an onerous burden if you entered into this with your eyes closed. Just think about these things and be aware.

SMOTHERING

Every once in a while you meet someone who has no life and is extremely lonely. Be glad you have met someone who will appreciate you. However, be careful that you don't lose all your freedom before you are ready. I call it "smothering" when you have a busy life plus liking time by yourself and this new person calls at least once a day and loves to talk and talk and talk, besides wanting to see you at least three times a week and generally takes up all your free time. Of course, it is up to you if you desire this kind of a relationship. Many Seniors have a life and want to continue to live it. They will make a bit of room for a new person but aren't willing to give up all their space. Give each other breathing room even if this is IT and sometimes even then! Once freedom is gone………

BUSINESS CARDS

When you are newly retired and finally settled in your new permanent residence, get some simple business cards made with your name, phone number and email on them. Whether you put your address on is a separate decision. Depends on how paranoid you are. I believe it isn't necessary. Does that mean I'm paranoid? Probably. But I tend to lean toward caution. I'm sure you don't want this person you just met showing up on your doorstep uninvited.

BLOOD TESTS

We discuss the necessity of this in another chapter and I cannot emphasize the importance enough if you are going to have a sexual relationship with a new person. Read the chapter Looking Forward to Sex.

PASSIVE AGGRESSIVE BEHAVIOR

If you haven't been in a relationship with a person with this personality trait, don't start now. The person seems so nice and always asks you where you want to go, where you want to stay, which movie you want to see, which people you want to go with, etc. As your relationship progresses it will concern which condo to buy, what furniture, which car, etc. And it always seems so thoughtful that he/she cares. Beware! When anything goes wrong or doesn't work out, who gets the blame? It's your fault because you made the decision. These situations and decisions shouldn't be the "blame kind" but with this type of personality, they are. And this is only one of the characteristics of passive-aggressive behavior. Just be cautious, share those decisions.

AGE AND OTHER DIFFERENCES

Is there something terribly wrong in dating a person of another generation? I don't think so, but there are pitfalls. One is old skin (being a woman I always think of that). Another is the older person's kids are the same age as you are, or maybe older! That can be tricky! These are only a couple of obvious differences but there are many, many more possibilities for problems. A generation gap is OK, but sometimes more difficult.

What I want to emphasize is, that a few years one way or the other doesn't make any difference. Male or female, it doesn't matter, I would hope. However, no matter the gender, hopefully, you are of the same generation and like the same music, have the same values, have experienced many of the same historic events and obviously these are all things you have in common, plus a whole lot more. It is easier to form a relationship with these common bonds.

Sometimes being raised in different parts of the country can be a problem as can race and religious differences. These problems are not always easy to solve but if you both try and consult others with similar problems or even seek professional counseling, if the relationship is tuning into a serious affair. Better nip these problems in the bud before they are fully blossomed and you have an elephant in the living room. Don't you think?

INTERNET DATING

This can be a fun thing if you are willing to go through all that it involves. There are some marvelous success stories out there as well as sad and disastrous ones. If you think you should try the Internet, by all means do it.

The same goes for ads in newspapers and other publications. Just follow the suggestions I made previously and don't get caught in some awful irrevocable mess. It sometimes seems that most of these people are really desperate and you're not. There are so many ways to meet new people if you follow some of my previous suggestions and ask your friends to help you with ideas and maybe even a blind date. Some say most men on the Internet are looking for sex and women are looking for rich men. Who knows? Just be careful.

BACKGROUND CHECKS

This can be tricky, but I highly recommend it if you personally do not know anything about him/her through family or friends. Also, if you have assets that you can't afford to lose. It's OK to be a tad suspicious and the other person probably is also. You got this far in life and have no desire to be suckered into a disastrous unknown. Swindled. So do a background check. It can be done on the Internet through People Search with a slight charge. Depending on circumstances a private detective could be a good choice. Ask your banker, lawyer, broker, insurance agent for a reference. But think how much more safe and secure you will feel if the "all clear" is given. Some of the most unscrupulous men/women are the best looking, most attractive, most romantic, most caring and most interesting people you'll ever meet. You never have to tell anyone you did this. Why should you unless it will help someone else? Just be sensible.

LENDING MONEY

Ditto! Ditto! Ditto! Recommend a bank to your acquaintance.

OPENESS

There is always something new to learn. Don't be a stick-in-the-mud and think the old ways are always the best. A few are, but a lot aren't. Be open to new things. Grow and enjoy!

Roger sent Kate an email before their first date, with chit chat and then he wrote, "I think you are very attractive and I am interested in occasional sex with you". Kate was quite surprised and frankly shocked at his forthrightness, but she liked Roger and went on the date anyway. They didn't discuss sex but found that they were even more interested in each other after spending some time together.

Kate realized then that she knew at least one of Roger's goals and decided she appreciated his frankness. She decided from the git go she knew where the relationship was headed if they clicked. It did click and they are both happy with the results.

When Kate told me about the beginning, I was startled as it was an unusual and surprising message even before the first date. However, it worked for them. It really does pay to be honest. With Roger and Kate, the proof was in the pudding!

MATES AND PARTNERS

"You can lead a horse to water but you can't make him drink"

"It's not what I say but what I mean"

OK, so here you are in a strange place, a new home to live in and a lifestyle to go with it.

If you have a mate or partner your route is quite different from the single seniors. You must always keep in mind that other person. And don't forget that. It's new to them, too. But on the other hand, your interests probably aren't identical so you both have to find some routes separately as well as commonalties that hopefully abound.

Computers have been mentioned before and I can't emphasize enough how helpful they can be to a relationship. You can look up anything. I suggest if neither of you is really up on computers that the male becomes the expert first. It's like driving the car. It suits them. Let the woman read the map and give the suggestions. Men are used to a job and often being in charge eventually. I don't mean to sound sexist about this but from what I have learned it is often the male who needs to find things to do to keep him happily occupied and out of his mate's hair. So my feeling is let them be the Head of Household as it says on the census. Some men need more help and direction now than others. Remember that computers are available to both of you. Get private lessons or group or whatever, just do it.

One of the things that I have enjoyed about my computer is the Bicycle Card Games disc I bought and installed. Sometimes I have half an hour or more to kill before I have an obligation. So I sit down and play a game of old fashioned Solitaire. Actually, I am addicted and without knowing it I can sit here for quite a long while and not realize how much time has passed. I think it's because I don't have to shuffle. It's so easy. And then the machine keeps track of your best times and you can't help but try to break your record. My best time winning is 1 minute 33 seconds! I can't believe it, but there it is and I'm not about to argue with the computer. Can you beat it? This is good entertainment & stimulation for both of you. And of course, there is Cribbage, Bridge, you name it. There is almost every card game and variations of each. It is fun and very relaxing.

E-mail is the industry's special gift to Seniors. You must do it to know how wonderful it is. When I send out postal letters, I try to remember to add my e-mail address. Eventually someday when you open your e-mail, there will be a letter from a friend who also has a computer. It's so much fun when that happens. I was very reluctant to get involved in e-mail because I just somehow knew it would take too much of my time – and it does, and I love it!

Is your mate a couch potato? Do you ever join him/her? Why not? Sports are great and if your mate enjoys them why don't you try to also? If there are games in town, attend. If it is baseball, learn to keep score. You'll learn the game that way. The finer points will come along the more games you attend.

How about football? Go to the games whether it be high school, college or the pros. Have a team, be loyal, show enthusiasm. I don't understand soccer but if my mate loved it, I would learn about it so we could share that pleasure. How about pool? Pool is a great sport to enjoy together but you must have patience and not get into that twisted thinking, which is discussed in another chapter. Croquet on the lawn is summer fun for a group or just the two of you to practice for a neighbor hood tournament.

And cards. I mentioned Solitaire on the computer but what about Pinochle or Cribbage with your mate. Bill & I used to play 3 games with real cards after each meal we ate at home together and kept a running score posted on the refrigerator. It was a good way for us to connect and enjoy our coffee after a meal together.

Way back when we were both working, my mate and I had a co-partnership arrangement in the kitchen. I prepared the meals and he cleaned up afterwards. I did basic stuff before I sat down to eat so he didn't face tornado damage after dinner and that made it easier for him and no big deal for me. This can be done the same or in reverse when you are retired. I think men like to be part of the kitchen, whether it's cooking or just being there, so try to share the responsibilities and see how it works. And girls, don't be so damn finicky and sneak around changing this and that after he is through. Just let it be & give him a loving hug and be grateful that he is with you.

Something else we need to be aware of is compliments. Now that you're not working and those pats-on-the-back aren't as forthcoming, you both need to fill the gap. How clean the car is, how nice the house looks, the garden looks lovely, look at those gorgeous geraniums, how great you look in that shirt, you look beautiful in that outfit, I loved dinner but the salad was especially good, you still barbecue the best chicken, I like your haircut, you're still so sexy, and thanks for doing the dishes and cleaning up the kitchen so nicely! It's so easy & so appreciated!

How about finally putting that scrapbook or photo album in order? It is so much fun to wade through all that stuff and reminisce together. You might be amazed at the different things you each remember in your own way. What a wonderful way to share yesterday, today and tomorrow. Turn off the damn TV once in a while and do things together!

This is also a good time to get all your papers in order, if you haven't already done that. Make some decisions about various possessions and who gets what. Do your will or a trust . Decide if you want a Physicians Directive and if so, do it. Be sure you let a neighbor or a nearby close relative know where these papers are in case of a calamity.

A good idea to remember is to make notes of important phone conversations that you have. Date them & file in the appropriate place. (Aren't you glad you kept the file cabinet?) I have discovered that some important dealings I have can not be discussed on the phone because there is no record of the conversations and I'm not quite sure of the other person's memory. So I either take detailed notes or we write back and forth or email so there can be no misunderstandings. Pam suggests you might think about using colored paper for these items. They can be found immediately in their proper file. You can use the same color for any notes so you don't have to have different colors around. You know what they are simply because they are on colored paper.

Decide with your kids or other family members what you prefer to have happen with your body when you die. I sometimes think that it is more important that your family be happy with what is done with your body than you are. They are the ones who are left for years to come and whether they visit a gravestone or think of you when they are at the beach because you had your ashes scattered at sea will be part of their lives, not yours. Check out possibilities like Neptune Society and different undertakers in the area. You'll feel so much more relaxed knowing these tasks have been handled and settled.

If you want to be an organ donor, now is the time to make that clear with a written directive. My Dad died from Alzheimer's and the family's wish was to donate any of his organs and especially his brain for research. But sadly, through poor communication with the nursing home this was not brought to their attention soon enough and his remains were carted away with no medical research ordered. That has always made me sad. His wish had been that maybe something would have been learned from our family tragedy and that maybe someone else would eventually benefit. Not to be. Sorry, Daddy.

There is something I have noticed about some married senior couples that I know. These are just normal average couples, not wife beaters or abusers, just ordinary people. Some of the men tend to bully their wives, sometimes in a gentle manner but not always. They try to disguise it with humor. It looks to me like such a put-down and I wonder, "how long has this been going on?" This was a totally new picture to me and I have been curious about it.

Some women feel that non-communication is another form of bullying. The wife is left completely in the dark about what her husband thinks of anything and everything. We hear about the nagging wife and the hen-pecked husband but what about the beaten-down wife in normal, "happy" marriages? It's all so subtle and I'm sure the husband isn't aware of what he is doing to his wife's self esteem, ego and image of herself. Then I wondered what nagging does to a husband's image of himself, ego and self-esteem? I have talked about this subject with women friends and they all say that it is such a gradual happening that you aren't aware of the erosion to your spirit and self esteem until you almost hit bottom, or are forced to be on your own. Then, Wham! It's like being hit in the gut with a shovel. Think about all that and don't fall into this pathetic pit, either one of you.

Something else I have noticed is the almost total non-acceptance by some mates of their partners aging process. He can't accept that she isn't as quick or as alert as she was and also can't accept the fact that he is aging and becomes very aggressive to the point of being verbally abusive. She can't accept the fact that she is a bit slower, more tired, etc. and that he is having the same trouble. This whole process can apply to either person. I used he's and she's only as an example. If one of you notices this happening in your relationship, seek some help.

I believe this is what happened to my friends, Lily and Donald, who are in their mid 80's. After over sixty years of marriage, Lily has moved into an Assisted Living place just to get away from Donald. She is so happy and relaxed now. It is wonderful to see. Poor Donald continues to be his old mean aggressive self and just will not seek any counseling. Lily went to the local Counsel on Aging seeking advice and got it, and then took it. It's sad but she feels safe now. If this happens in your life, do something about it. No one needs verbal abuse. Sometimes it's as simple as accepting where you and your partner are in life. That word "accepting" is such a big word.

We all have disagreements and it is important how we argue. We have to remember that there might not be a tomorrow and to be careful how we have discussions or "committee meetings" (as a friend calls them). The big trouble makers are: 1) Criticism, 2) Defensiveness, 3) Contempt, and 4) Withdrawal. Try to avoid falling into those verbal and aggressive traps.

One important thing that unfortunately happens to most of us is: forgetting! We all have heard about it and probably have noticed it ourselves or possibly someone has said to you, "we talked about that yesterday" or "I already explained that to you". Believe me, phrases like that are devastating to hear more than once. Be kind, and let your mate mention again something to you. Being patient with each other is so very important. I'm talking now of just ordinary living day to day without senility being involved.

If senility or Alzheimer's creeps into your lives, I highly recommend the book, "The 36 Hour Day". It is fantastic in its explanation of that particular aging disease and how one can cope with it oh, so much easier. The methods of communication I learned reading that book helped me so much when my Dad had Alzheimers. The patience I learned from that fabulous book helped me cope with my daughter's temporary memory loss after she was in a car accident and asked me every 10 minutes for a few weeks, "what happened to me?" It is a wonderful gift for a friend or for yourself

Over the years I have noticed senior couples in restaurants having dinner and seldom saying a word to each other. I think it's because they are used to watching TV while they eat and have forgotten some of the pleasures of conversation. I always felt so badly for them and wondered about it. I swore this would never happen to me. Maybe married people have talked everything over & over and have nothing left to say to each other. I don't believe that. There has to be a way around this. When you're single and going out with a friend there seems to be plenty of topics to explore. So here's what you both do. While you're getting ready to go out, each of you thinks of three topics for discussion during dinner and then you take turns initiating a topic. The partner has to respond and participate as you do. Listen to the words and reply accordingly. Try it! Soon the evening is over and you realize you have only discussed 4 of the 6 topics.

Sometimes when Mary & Buck were out, Mary would become aware that their table was silent and everyone around them was laughing and apparently enjoying themselves. This is what Mary invented: Mary would say, "1 - 2 - 3", and happily laugh a bit. Buck would then reply, "4 - 5 - 6" , and laugh uproariously. This would continue until they reached 10 and by then the conversation bug had once again captured their attention! It's such a silly thing, but fun. I dare you to give it a shot!

People who eat alone all the time tend to get a bit lax with their table manners. Then when he/she is out, they are either confused, belligerent, or reticent to start eating. It is so easy to fall into this trap. If you are reading or watching TV with your elbows on the table and stuffing your face like there was no tomorrow, or worse yet, just standing at the kitchen counter fulfilling the eating obligation, you are going to get lazy about some of the niceties of our mores. Don't fall into this habit. Sit down, put a napkin in your lap, and keep your elbows off the table, just like you tell the grandkids.

Once in a while Senior Onset Alcoholism rears its ugly head. It is not uncommon. A drink before dinner is nice, or wine with dinner is nice, and a little cognac or port is a treat after dinner. But be careful. It doesn't have to be every night. If it does, you better think about it and do without once in a while. When you do have a drink of alcohol, use a jigger to measure. Don't just pour it in and don't let your mate do so either. You can't control your mate so don't try. Just be wise. And don't drink at lunch. Once one of you is hooked, your lovely well-planned and contented life goes to hell. The alcoholic can only help himself/herself. The other party can go to Al-Anon for help, counseling and inspiration. Buy their book One Day at a Time and read it daily for inspiration. The best advice is: live so that alcohol is a treat in your home not a habit or necessity. "What's done is done" is the way it is and you will have to figure out how to live with or without the other person if alcoholism comes into your life.

Different life styles seem to promote Senior Onset Alcoholism. While in the business world, one mate may have had many client lunches with drinks. A lot of us go out for lunch with friends and have a drink before lunch or wine with the meal, or play golf in the morning and then have a few at the 19th hole. No matter what the event, we go home and often take a nap. Naturally. First thing you know, it is cocktail time and whether you are alone or with friends, you're on your way once again. It's such an easy pattern or habit to get into. Just be aware and save your life and your relationship. Don't get into the habit.

Be sure to remember about romance. We all love it and you know it. Read the chapter on Sex. There are also some good ideas in Do's And Don'ts of Dating. It's never too late to show affection and love to and for your mate or partner. Lots of caring thoughts and good luck!

Here's a toast for you and your partner:
    Here's to the Ability
    To have the Agility
    To take our Virility
    Into our Senility!

APPEARANCE

"Pretty is as pretty does"

WARDROBE

"If you would only act as nice as you look"
"If a man's socks are pulled up, he is a gentleman"
(I hope you don't believe that)

Do you dress like your Mom or your Grandmother? Honestly, some people (both sexes) just can't seem to be in style or even close. And I don't mean current fads or "fashion". There are certain traditional looks that are classic and never go out of style. But the ones I'm talking about never were in style. But don't go to the other extreme either like your too-with-it grandchild. Jeez!

Polyester pants/slacks worn with a polyester over blouse were never smart or in style. It just was so easy it seems to me. My used-to-be dapper friend, Molly, says she is so sloppy when she eats that she has given up wearing silk or linen because she has to have every thing dry cleaned after wearing it only once. Give me a break. We all spill and make a mess once in a while. Eat slower! Tuck a napkin in the neck of your shirt! Put a napkin in your lap! Watch your meal companions dribble and afterwards they will see that you are all neat & tidy. Guess who will change their ways?

Don't give up silk and linen and cotton. They have style and class and set you apart as a smart person with pizzazz and fashion sense. Besides looking good those fabrics also make you feel better. Check the label and see if the garment is washable. I don't mean for us to be snobby but we don't have to be disgustingly sloppy either. I think a goal could be: Look gracious and dress smartly.

I definitely believe in sweat pants, sweat shirts and big old T-shirts with advertising on them or maybe a souvenir from a favorite trip. Wear them around the house, garage, yard and so forth, but don't always go every place in them. You can still be comfortable in clothes with a bit of style. You don't want to be so easily recognizable as that grumpy old man or lady from down the street. "You can always tell them by their dirty, stained and fat clothes". Show some pride and make them think instead, "Now that's an interesting looking older person".

This seems a good place to mention hanging on to some of the clothes of my deceased parents. I love my Dad's sweat pants and long sleeve with-collar golf sweaters. I wear those a lot and they make me feel good and they fit comfortably. I naturally kept my Mom's jewelry and delight in wearing her earrings and necklaces. And I always carry one of her beaded bags to the opera or symphony. My favorite cold weather outer garment outfit is Mom's navy blue cashmere coat, my Dad's black scarf and a navy stocking cap that my Grandma knit. I couldn't feel warmer or more loved. What a nice outfit to have.

Soft commercial knits are such wonderful fabrics. They are flexible and expand and give where necessary. They are a delight to wash and wear often with no ironing. Some are cool and others are snuggly when you need that warmth. I must mention the down side of knit pants for women. Often they are too tight and your butt looks just awful. There is no other way to describe it. Loose is much better than tight. If you heard some of the comments that are made, I swear you would never wear too tight stretch pants again. There can be a negative side to men wearing these comfortable knit pants also. They need to wear fitted shorts (like Jockeys) with them, never boxers, please.

Hey men, once you get rid of that big fat gut you can wear some handsome slacks with a great looking shirt. If you still have that gut, please don't wear a shirt that buttons down the front because inevitably it will stretch open across your hairy belly as undershirts never seem to be long enough to cover that extra large portion and you will look gross. Men also should think about how they look when they tuck a shirt in, around and over that big protrusion of a stomach. Tucking in just accents it. Take a tip from some of the smart women around and wear your shirt outside your britches. Your wife or prospective women and all your friends deserve a more presentable companion. A big, fat stomach can be such a distraction.

And one more thing if you are a big fat slob, please make sure your pants are big enough to go around your waist or not too big so that when you stoop down, your behind doesn't peek at us out of your britches. Yuck! Crack Attack! (A diet could be the answer)

A really good thing about polyester is that it doesn't need to be ironed and that is wonderful. Buy other fabrics with a slight blend of polyester for convenience. No ironing is nice. But 100% polyester eventually will not wash clean and you will have dribble spots all over your shirts and pants. Ugh. So toss all those miserable, seedy looking shirts and pants.

There is a product called Redox (used to be Biz) that can be used on good clothing that is stubbornly and badly soiled. You can use a large dishpan with little water and one large scoop of Redox. If you have several stained items and are using the washer, use a minimum amount of water and 2 scoops of Redox. Try it. Pam says it is a wonder.

A decent pair of well fitting jeans with a tucked in shirt is always attractive for both sexes. And to dress it up, wear a blazer. Women wear a pair of low heels and men wear some other shoes besides sneakers, please! It's amazing how a pair of leather shoes or even clean canvas shoes can dress up the most casual outfit. Add a sweater over your shoulders or a blazer and Voila! ready for a movie, or lunch or dinner.

Sneakers are great. They support your feet and are the shoe for long walks. But, there are other shoes in this world. You might be surprised how comfortable you can be plus how spiffy you look in other types of shoes.

Ladies, when you buy Knee-highs, please be sure that is what you buy. Don't purchase Ankle-highs. They are the worst and look awful when you sit down in a pair of slacks and your leg above your ankles and elastic ridge show. I mean, why are you wearing hose in the first place? It's good advice!

One of the things that I don't care for about my body is that floppy flab that hangs from my upper arm. It used to be pretty and smooth and looked great in sleeveless blouses, shirts and dresses. Not anymore. If you think it looks OK, it doesn't. Please, wear long sleeves or long short sleeves. Just don't appear in a public place with those ugly upper arms showing. Please. It is not a pleasant sight.

As long as we're on the subject of ugly skin. Please don't wear those little short necklaces around your neck or over a sweater. Unless you have had the perfect cosmetic surgery on your neck, all that little doodad is going to do is draw attention to your neck skin. Right?

So wear the ones that hang down to your perky bosom. Let the people look at that!

Purses. Why do women always carry a purse? Is there a rule? I have asked so many women and the answers are all the same: "I have to have my wallet, my ID, my pills just in case, my make-up, my Kleenex container (plus hanky), my keys, a comb & brush, extra glasses, etc. etc. etc." ad nauseum. I can't believe what women cram into those purses and walk all over with them hanging on their arm or over their shoulder, but mostly over their arm. Every woman's self defense class I have ever attended says, "Get rid of your purse". You are an older woman walking around asking to be a victim. Right! A victim!

True story. Fern got some money from the ATM machine, rushed to catch her bus and just stuck the wad in her purse as she boarded the bus. Unknown to her, a trio of kids had been watching her and got on the bus at the same time. One sat across from her and one sat just behind her while the third one stood. The kid across from Fern made a huge scene with the boy behind her and while Fern was watching them, the boy standing reached into her purse and grabbed the loose wad of bills and jumped off the bus which had stopped as previously planned. The other two got off the bus and none of them was ever seen again. All because of that damn purse.

Try folding your paper money once & fasten with a giant size paper clip. Put your driver's license and one credit card in the paper clip with the money. And put it in one pants pocket with your small ring of house keys (and car if you're driving). One time I was having lunch at an outdoor cafe and happened to notice my keys on the ground. They had somehow fallen out of my pocket. When I got home I put a medium size safety pin on my key ring and now I pin it in my pocket as soon as I lock the door. That was such an easy lesson to learn. The pin comes in handy also when I walk in the morning before breakfast and can pin my keys to the waistband of my sweat pants.

In the other pocket put a handkerchief and drop in any pills you might need, like a breath mint or anything medical that you must have. A small pocket comb fits nicely in that same pocket. So that's it. Some pants have a rear pocket or two where the comb and maybe a small wallet will fit.. Unless you are going to be gone for hours & hours, you don't need your make-up. Do a good job before you start out. It will be fine.

There's often the problem of a couple bulkier items like a cell phone, a pager, or a Palm product. That's what so great about jeans and lots of khaki brands and corduroy in the winter. They have those two rear pockets where maybe your phone & pager will fit Key word in that sentence is "maybe". Sometimes there just isn't room so try using a clip-on for your belt or waistband. Cargo pants are handy for sure with those big roomy pockets. They may not fit your style but it is an idea. A fanny pack has space also. But think about it. Do you really need all three of those items every time you leave your home? I don't think so. Try leaving them and see what happens! Just try once in a while. You might enjoy the peace and freedom.

Let's talk about glasses. It's OK to wear them. So wear them. Don't stick them in that purse you shouldn't be carrying and drag them out every time you want to read a menu or a price tag. Or then drag out another pair that is your fashion statement sunglasses. Years ago I decided that if I had to wear the damn things, that was what I was going to do and not let them rule my life. Put them on in the morning and take them off when I go to bed. And it's great. But you have to get trifocals and you can get them so they don't have those ugly horizontal lines through them. They are called multi-focal progressive. Trifocals are for 1) reading, 2) viewing the computer or library bookshelves and, 3) distance. You might find at first that you get dizzy or headachy. The problem is scanning. You must learn to look at one place and then another. Do Not scan from one spot to another. Look here, then look there.

To top off the perfect pair of glasses, you have to get the kind that gets dark when you are outdoors. They are called photo chromatic or Transitional, which is a brand name. With some styles you can get extra, extra strong clip-on sunglasses for special occasions like the beach or car trips when the ordinary is not quite dark enough. Sun sensitive glasses are so convenient and I love them, plus, they cover up quite a bit of those circles (and sometimes bags) under my eyes. The styles are very fashionable so you don't really look like your grandmother. Hey, that could be me!

Now, isn't that easy without a purse? It may take a few days to get used to it but it works. When I go grocery shopping I stick my list in the money clip & take a little golf pencil along to cross off items. You can do this. You will feel safer and you won't look like a victim waiting to happen.

However, there is a big but here about purses, and that is a huge hooray for fanny packs. If you are going on a long walk, a short hike, a picnic, anything like that, a fanny pack is what you need. They come in different fabrics and colors and are so very convenient and give you a feeling of security. Make sure you wear it tight enough so if someone were to cut it in the back you would be aware of it leaving you, then yell like crazy.

Shoulder bags could be the answer to the purse problem for you. If you take one, put it over one shoulder and over your head so that a "grabber thief" can't yank it off your shoulder and run off down the street. Be cautious and wise. Sometimes it's mean out there. Ask Fern, she knows and now carries a shoulder bag over her head & shoulder.

Something I discovered in having to carry my lunch, thermos, work papers, etc. are tote bags. When they have two long handles you can maneuver around so that you have put your arms through the handles and on to your shoulders so it is hanging down your back like a backpack. It may look a bit weird but it isn't killing your arm and the weight is evenly distributed making it very easy to "tote" for endless blocks. I'm hoping that one day someone will design a classy backpack for us Seniors. In the meantime, try my idea.

Does your locale have a discount store that handles the "can't sell" or "unsold clearance items from a big department store? Nordstrom's has one called The Rack and it is a wonderful place to shop. The bargains for shoes & clothes are amazing for both sexes.

Have you discovered second-hand stores yet? Especially the ones with clothes on consignment? What bargains you can buy there. My friend Molly, from back east, was so delighted to find a $400 dress for $75 and then she actually bargained them down to $50. And my friend Kathleen from Northern California was ecstatic with her purchases. I have found sweaters, jackets, and pants. I just bought a great pair of aqua linen shorts for $3.50. I have already mentioned to check out Goodwill & those kinds of shops for items like T-shirts, sweat shirts, jeans, pants, and jackets. You might be amazed. Great for a tight budget. Between the give-away shelves in the laundry room, second hand, and consignment shops I have done all right! You can too.

I must mention the handy and useful big shirts I have found. Sometimes they are called camp shirts and are worn on the outside over a T-shirt or blouse, not tucked in like normal shirts. I think of them as warm-weather jackets. They usually have a straight across hem with no tails. However, there are some with tails that are of wonderful fabric like linen, corduroy, or wool that look terrific as an over shirt. You can tell because they have style. They are very nice for a movie just to have a little extra covering in the air conditioning. Also, they tie around the waist nice 'n easy if you are walking. I found some of mine in second hand stores: a black heavy silk and a washed out blue of the same fabric and a beige & white striped linen shirt and a plain beige one. They look so great.

A couple years ago I discovered that many of my slacks/pants/skirts/shorts that had elastic waists were kaput. The elastic was shot and totally useless. And being the conservative person that I am I couldn't toss out these good items just because the waist wasn't there anymore. After much belaboring over this dilemma, I decided to cut out the elastic and fold over the waist and put in drawstrings. I bought the metal circle inserts and clamped them on and put in the drawstrings. I shopped at a good fabric store and was able to get different colors for my different needs. It worked out really well & I am content. Still have the outfits that I like plus a bonus: a little weight change here 'n there isn't a big deal!

I had my colors done several years ago when I was in my 40's and learned I was a Spring. I liked being a Spring. It had a nice ring to it. What I took from it was that white and black were no-no's for me. I realized that there was too much contrast for my skin and black or white weren't flattering at all to my coloring. So my two basic colors became navy blue and off-white or egg shell and I accessorized with almost all the other colors. I liked the assurance of knowing my colors were right for me and I looked my best in them.

When I was 66 and moved up here, my dear friend, Jessica, gave me a gorgeous black, very dressy, pants outfit to wear to the opera. So here I was with this free lovely outfit and not one accessory. No shoes, no wrap, nada. So I bought shoes and made a fringed shawl. Then my volunteer work at the museum for a special travelling exhibit required me to wear black slacks, so I bought those plus more suitable shoes than the ones for the opera. One thing led to another and I am once again wearing black and I like it and am comfortable in the color. Navy blue is almost extinct for me now except for a casual denim suit that is still perfect for many occasions. Funny how we change. Be open to these events in your life. You never know what's around the corner.

Men, don't forget about the socks. It might give you "sox appeal".

HAIR & MAKE-UP

"Squeaky hair is clean hair"

"You're only as old as you think

Believe me when I say I don't want to hurt anyone's feelings. The following hints and ideas come from observations over the years from friends and from me. People chatter and gossip about this stuff. I want you to start your new life with all the pluses you can muster so that you will have a great retirement. Please bear with me while I air some of these thoughts. And please use what applies to you. Good luck and thanks!

It is amazing to me how many men & women who have had naturally black hair and are starting to turn grey, dye their hair jet black. Don't they know that the grey is softening for their aging skin? There has got to be some other way. How about streaking and lightening it with grey? Or even dyeing it a dark brown with some subtle lighter streaks in it? Just don't do the black dye job with that reddish purple scalp that happens sometimes.

Often it looks maroon or burgundy or merlot if you're into wine. It only lasts a couple of weeks and it is so noticeable as it grows out. It is obvious and unattractive and harsh. Often it looks like a wig or hairpiece. That soft grey color is flattering to the skin. I do sympathize with the black hair people. I understand why they don't like it because it shows that they are getting old in a way strange and unfamiliar to them. And they don't recognize themselves with odd shade surrounding their faces. So, big deal. Everyone knows you're getting older and it's OK. Accept it. It ain't gonna change. If you feel you are too young to be grey, that is totally understandable. However, grey hair can be beautiful and very flattering. Plus, if you have great posture and dress smartly and are a today person, who cares? Flatter the grey. Use it for all its worth. Go for it and enjoy!

Now blondes also have a problem. Not the same but similar. Their natural blonde hair has to turn brown before it can turn that natural ashy, grey blonde or golden white. My mother ended up with the prettiest hair and I hope I will be as fortunate. When my hair started to darken and turn brown I was in my late 50's. I would look in the mirror and wonder who that was. I would have been pleased to be going grey but brown hair framing this blonde face was not me. It was dark and much too contrasting and was creating the opposite effect that would be flattering. So I started getting it woven every couple of months. I could afford it then. I discovered that the coloring gave my hair body for the first time and wasn't its usual old limp stuff.

Now I'm over 70 and can't afford that $80 luxury anymore. But more importantly, I don't have to be a blonde anymore. And just like those brunettes, I am also growing old. So I have it cut quite short and am content because some of it (near my face) has turned golden white and that's fine with me. I can't see the back of my head, so who cares if it is an oldish brown-blonde. I don't mean to offend any brunettes out there. You guys have great thick luxurious hair. I don't. When I was a natural blonde kid, you were jealous of me, not knowing that to me, your hair was fabulous.

You know how men have been using Rogaine for years and apparently being quite satisfied. At least I haven't heard any complaints except they have to keep using it for the rest of their lives. Gee, isn't that a shame? My friend Kathleen, has been using Rogaine for Women for a couple of years now and what a beautiful head of white hair that women has. It's gorgeous. So gals, if you are getting a bald spot or two, give it a try. You can always quit, but if you are pleased then you must continue using as the directions say. Personally, I think for women of any age it is a good deal.

And speaking of the backs of our heads. Use a hand mirror once in a while to check it out before you leave your home. Often a cowlick and other funny things have happened to your hair while you were sleeping or just leaning back in that comfy chair and need to be fixed. You may look great from the front but the back of your head can be a giggle.

What do you think about wigs and toupees? I think the wig makers need to look at real life senior men and women and carefully inspect some heads of hair. They usually don't have a big, thick mass of hair. I would think that one of the purposes of wearing a wig would be to look natural, unless you are a performer. Well, most of the wigs and toupees I have seen, not all but most, absolutely do not look like any senior hair I know. Can they be thinned? Ask & try it. When the wigs and toupees are right, they look wonderful and no one can tell where you end and they begin. And isn't that the point?

Do any of you still wear your hair long? Do you fling it around and over your shoulders like the young sexpots? I hope not. To me, long hair on an old face is a downer. We need to wear our hair short and get a perky up-lifting look rather than the long, straight dragged down look. Even waved it is not flattering. It's amazing to me that someone in their 60's or more can still try to wear their hair like they did in high school. Why? It is unflattering and often foolish or silly. Be your age and proud of it. Look smart.

Sometimes there isn't much to talk about hair because there isn't much hair there! However, men, when you are in the process of getting a sexy bald spot on the top of your head, let it become just that. Please, don't part your hair down by your ear and then comb over the top of your head the few long strands you can find. Please don't do that. It really looks dumb. Some men even shave their heads to achieve that handsome bald look. You don't have to go that far, just be yourself. Forget parting it and just wear your hair trimmed normally. Thank you!

And one more thing for the guys. What do you think of grey haired men wearing a shaggy ponytail? I'm not sure how I feel. Is it appropriate? Is it profiling artists and musicians? Or is it just a comfortable style? Don't you find it tedious to cope with snarls & long hair? I think we all have to be in a style that is right and comfortable for each of us. Enjoy.

OK girls! How do you put on make-up? I can't believe the antics that some of us pursue just to put on a bit of eyeliner and mascara. It's so silly. All that squinting and hoping for the best. Buy a stick-on magnifying mirror and put it at a comfortable height on your bathroom mirror. You will love it! At first, everyone says, "Ooh, how can you stand to look at yourself so close up?" It's not so bad and certainly better than missing the target half the time or smearing your eyes all up and taking twice as long as necessary. I believe I got my mirror at Brookstone, but I have seen them lately in other places. It's the best.

Men may josh you about the magnifying mirror but once used for a ticklish project like clipping nose or ear hair, they are sold. Nothing is better for trimming a moustache or the finer points of a beard. Trust me. Wonder if they sell His & Hers Mirrors?

Make-up should be adjusted gently as we age. Our eyes don't look the same since we usually are wearing glasses. They partially hide our eyes and the age evidence under them. I feel that false eyelashes are passe. And that bright, bold eyeliner doesn't do much to enhance our eyes anymore. Rouge, cheek color, blush should be soft and gentle and nice to you. Wear make-up but be content to tone everything down and glow from within!

A thought about lipstick. Most women's lips tend to get thinner as they get older. My theory is they get that way from women gritting their teeth and biting their tongues throughout the years. Sometimes it seems as if some women's mouths have just disappeared. There isn't much we can do except accept it and get on with our lives. Since your mouth is decidedly different than it was in your youth don't you think you should adjust the amount of lipstick you wear? Wear ever so much less and not those loud vivid colors that draw everyone's attention to your pinched lips. Please.

"Less is more"

BIRTHDAY UNDERWEAR

"If you don't try it, you'll never know if you can do it or not"

"Always wear clean underwear in case you are in an accident"

On my 70th birthday, I threw away all my bras and panties! I had made an appointment with a professional fitter in the lingerie department of our major department store and was there on time for the fitting.

The whole thing was an exhilarating experience. Maybe a tad embarrassing at first but once I saw the difference, I was hooked (literally). I don't think I had ever had a professional fitting so it was all new and very educational. Pat, the expert, wedged me, molded me, and shook me into all the styles and types there were until we found the ones that fitted my desires and me the best.

My breasts aren't big but they are part of my femininity and I wanted them to be somewhat up and out there. None of this letting them just hang and looking totally inconspicuous anymore. I am a vital, energetic woman and wanted to look and feel that way. Amazing how much our breasts have to do with our self-image. The fitter agreed with me.

I told Pat that I didn't wear low-neck dresses anymore. My "chest" skin is shot from too much sun in my other years and I see no point in pushing up and brandishing that dried and wrinkly skin. To me, it is ugly. Also I didn't want that padded stuff. I just wanted bras that fit, uplifted and molded me into my nice feminine self. I have the breasts. It's just that they aren't where they could be.

With Pat's help, I chose six skin colored bras and two black ones! Oh yes! Definitely want to have black when wearing a darker blouse or sweater. Besides it makes you feel sexy and fun! I didn't select any white because it shows too clearly through almost any garment you wear. I chose a variety of styles to test for a year and would give away the ones that somehow didn't work out. That was probably extravagant but hey, it's my birthday!

And then the panties. Don't buy those ugly big cotton things that look like a laundry bag and make you appear to be about that same size. If the crotch has the cotton lining you are getting all the benefits you need. I had been wearing hip huggers for years but this time decided to dispense with the normal elastic waistband and go with a very wide lacey waistband. It's about two inches and doesn't pinch. I found just what I wanted in a comfortable hip hugger style that is made by Olga, as are most of the bras. And I bought mostly skin color but naturally had to get some black for those black outfits! The panties cover my navel and my lower 3-children-later tummy. I'm pleased to say that when I am in only my underwear, my waistline really shows. I frankly don't expect to ever be "involved" with another man again but I still like to feel good about myself. That's part of our self- esteem. Even if my skin is kinda ucky I still look curvy and in a dim light I pass my own harsh critical appraisal.

I remember several years before my Dad died, he said to me in a very wistful way, "I haven't seen your Mother naked in many years now." I felt so sad for him knowing how much he adored her but since she had gained weight and her skin wasn't as pretty as it had been, she was more private about her appearance. Sometimes there are other people who care and it is sad when our bodies and our self images change. Keep in mind that we are the only ones in charge of ourselves. Do a good job. Be generous and kind to yourself. Who else is? I don't mean that in a selfish way. Just be aware and wise. We have earned everything we have! Happy Birthday!!

A few of my younger, skinny friends wear thongs. I thought about trying them but decided that panty liners just didn't go with a thong! And oh yeah, panty liners became a part of my life this past year. I like them. You throw away the liner and wear the panties another day. Saves lots of wear & tear on panties by less laundering. Get used to comfy panty liners. They are practically a necessity and such a relief when you sneeze or cough. Believe me.

A week or so later after being carefully scrutinized by some of my friends, one chubby, older friend bosom-at-her-waist said, "Well, look at you! What's happened? " I told her. Next time I saw her, she was wearing a low neck something or other with her breasts practically under her chin and asked me what I thought. I smiled and said, "Wow!" Believe me, don't go that route. It looks silly and not especially attractive on older women. Decide your goal.

I had lost ten pounds prior to my birthday and then unintentionally lost another ten pounds in the next few months. Oh well, what the hell, it's gone and I didn't suffer. So I had to give away what seemed to be the bigger bra styles and just kept the ones that fit the best. I went back to check with Pat and she helped me to decide. I mean she's the expert. I ended up keeping four and both the black ones, which are still perfect! Hint: Wait until you have attained any planned weight loss before buying bras. The panties were still perfect. I hadn't planned that extra ten pounds but I was delighted and still am. And I had a great Birthday! I didn't mind being 70, but it was difficult to accept being a septuagenarian. I mean, really! (After thought: And now I actually look forward to being an octogenarian. It will come soon enough. Much better than the alternative.)

I talked about this chapter with a friend, Lily, who recently had a breast removed because of cancer. It's still so new to her and she's not sure how she feels anymore. Another friend, Mary, had a breast removed, then had an implant and tattooing for a nipple. She is all for anything that makes you feel comfortable and like yourself. I hope Lily will feel like that as she is further along in her recovery. These women were dealt a dirty deal and you can't get around that. In various ways we all have had our dirty deals but eventually you have to press on, or wither and die. I prefer living!

COSMETIC SURGERY

"Too many cooks spoil the soup"
"Character is a victory not a gift"

I must talk about cosmetic surgery for a bit. Do it. If you can afford it, don't hesitate. But some words of caution. I think the most important thing is to remember that it is not going to change your life. It is only going to enhance your image of yourself and possibly help you to be yourself. Cosmetic surgery is expensive but worth it if you can live with the reality of what you have done. Don't be fooled into thinking it is the panacea of all your dreams. It is like a good make-up job. It is permanent for a few years only. Are we agreed? If not, read the paragraph again until you understand.

I think the simplest cosmetic surgery is the removal of moles or spots that look like they could become cancerous. Don't delay. Do it for your peace of mind. I think people that leave big old warts or moles on their faces are weird. I don't understand that thinking. I go to a dermatologist for "spot" removal. Usually Dr. Tavelli freezes them and it's almost painless. I had one that he needed to make an incision to remove and fortunately, it was benign. This isn't always the case with every one, so don't take chances. And make sure the Doctor checks your back. You never know what could be growing there.

When Bill & I lived in San Mateo and ran our restaurant, The Dining Room, I was the manager and matre d'. Bill was a waiter and assistant to the chef for all sorts of stuff during the day and of course helped me manage. We became good friends with some of the steady clientele and it was fun to sit with them after hours and drink wine and talk about whatever. When I was 48 a couple of the patrons asked me, "Why are you angry? You look so unhappy." I hadn't even noticed but I did then. And what I noticed was that the skin over my eyes was drooping down, and they were right, I did look angry and tired. That wasn't me. I was a happy soul and who was this angry looking person?

So I checked out a plastic surgeon and had a Blepharoplasty performed. It was all worth it when after I was healed, my husband looked at me with his dimples and big grin and said, "I had forgotten what big blue eyes you had". I highly recommend that surgery. It stood me in good stead for many years and I don't regret one dollar of the cost. So if in your eyes, you have a gigantic physical blemish, fix it. It will restore your self-esteem. I never feel I look pissed off at the world anymore! Sometimes I feel like Mary Tyler Moore in her TV show when she turned the world on with a smile.

And one more before retirement story that applies to how I feel today. I was probably 55 when I went to a Spa after a very exhausting tax season to recuperate for a week. As usual they had special speakers and programs in the evening to do with health, beauty, exercise and general well being. This particular night the speaker was going on about make-up and I volunteered to be a guinea pig for her demonstration. So I got up in front of this group of probably 20 strangers (fortunately) and she said, "You have the body of a 30 year old, the face of a 40 year old, and the neck of a 80 year old!" How would you feel? That was all it took. I wasn't out of there a week and had another appointment with the plastic surgeon. And my neck finally got in line with the rest of me. It was worth every dollar and I shall continue to support those two surgeries.

There are many other cosmetic surgeries available today. If you don't know a surgeon's work personally, please ask your knowledgeable friends and/or your physician. You can get rid of those flabby arms, your tummy fat or that cellulite on your hips. Implants are available but I am guessing that in most cases we aren't interested in new breasts. But, hey, with breast cancer and other ills, one never knows. Two of my friends have each had a breast removed and one got an implant and the other didn't. They are both content with their decision. Just remember, cosmetic surgery isn't going to change who you are. We must learn to be content with our age and ourselves. Sometimes that is the hardest part.

It scares and horrifies me when I see some of the full-lifts that are done on wonderful women. There is no reason to have your face so contorted that your mouth and your smile stretch from ear to ear. And then your nose gets pulled all out shape, which requires more surgery. Please, use some discretion with plastic surgery. Accept that you will never look 40 again, but that you can look better than angry at 80 when you are only 50 or 60. Be cautious and make certain that the surgeon understands what you want & that he doesn't go bananas on the only face that you have. Best of luck!!

EATING PLANS

"If you start something, finish it"

INFORMATION

"A stitch in time saves nine"

The toughest part of dieting is keeping that lost weight off, but first you have to lose it. Period. If your goal is more than the diet "promises", take a break of at least a week or maybe two or even longer before restricting yourself so much again. You will notice that you do NOT lose as much the second time as you did the first. Keep at it. Don't give up. You WILL reach your goal one way or the other, if you persist. If you have any health problems you should discuss any drastic change in your eating habits with your doctor.

Do it!

A word about doctors. So often they pooh pooh diets. They just say, "eat healthy and exercise". Fine, let them, but we know you have to get there first. So be frank with your physician and tell her/him what you are going to do it and want his help and opinion. Test his knowledge by mentioning your BMI. And be sure to mention Vitamins and any Supplements that you take like Glucosamine for Arthritis, etc. You'll feel better knowing that you are doing an OK thing. Really!

Here's how to measure what your body mass index (BMI) is. Knowing that, will help you figure where you are and maybe help you to decide how much to lose or to stay the same.

Step 1. Multiply your weight in pounds by 703
Step 2. Multiply your height in inches by itself.
Step 3. Divide the first number by the second.

Round to the nearest whole number. That's your Body Mass Index. And it means:

BMI under 19 - Underweight
BMI 19 to 25 - Healthy weight
BMI 26 to 30 - Overweight
BMI 31 to 39: Very overweight
BMI 40 & above: Extremely overweight

Now make your weight decisions. I will show you how to keep it off after we talk about losing it. Forget about belonging to the Clean Plate Club. It's not necessary anymore and besides that's probably how you got to be overweight in the first place! Or if it's so ingrained in you as it is in me, just dish up smaller portions (which is what you should have been doing all along). Remember, you are in charge.

Idea: If you don't want to do a strict diet you might be interested in the counting of calories as a method of losing excess weight. I use that to maintain but it can be used for losing also. If you choose to do that, skip to the section, "Keeping It Off". Good luck!

DIETING

"Keep doing what you're doing and you'll get what you're getting"

"You can lead a horse to water but you can't make him drink"

"A watched pot never boils"

"There's No Free Lunch"

There are many, many available diets out there. I have tried some and scoffed at others. Now, as a senior, I go back to my roots, copy my Grandma, and thank her!

My Grandma's back and side yard was a huge garden. Her pride and joy were her strawberries but her "way of life" was vegetables that she grew and that was what I ate when I visited. What I didn't know until much later in my life was that was how she maintained her weight, health and shapely body. I can still remember eating one of her vegetable soup concoctions and loving it. Later in our relationship I learned that she made her soups without any meat products or fat and when the scales showed her numbers she didn't like, she would just make a huge pot of soup, eat it three times a day until it was gone. One meal a day she would have a piece of fruit, or a chicken breast, or maybe even a very lean pork chop but that was it.

I didn't realize the genius of my Grandma until I was in my late 20's & felt too round after three pregnancies! I mentioned my problem in a letter to her & she reminded me of her soup. I wish I still had that letter but I don't, so the next best thing is to share her diet with you with a few additions not always available to Grandma.! It gets boring but that's OK because it really works & is worth the free time you gain! And the weight you lose!

> Sliced carrots
> A bunch of celery sliced
> Sliced spinach
> Sliced head of cabbage
> Big yellow onion sliced or a bunch of scallions
> Big can of tomato juice (or V-8 juice) or big can of diced tomatoes
> Sliced Mushrooms (a luxury for Grandma)
> Frozen green beans (hers were fresh)
> Sliced beet greens
> Any other vegetable greens you might favor may be added
> Salt & pepper and any other seasonings you choose

(In later years years, I have added a package of French onion soup & bouillon cubes

Add enough water to cover, bring to boil, simmer 30 minutes. Let it sit overnight, scoop a ladle full & heat in a small pan for breakfast & you're on your way!

That's it! And it does work. Be sure to drink a quart of water each day. But no booze, wine or beer. For one or two weeks you will lose 10 – 15 pounds! And don't be lazy!

LOU'S SAMPLE MEALS

"Don't cry over spilled milk"

"What about The Clean Plate Club?"

Here are some ideas. Read food labels and the Calorie counter book for more information. Some of the amounts may be off a bit but they are darn close.

Breakfast options
- Poached egg 70, on toast 100, grapefruit juice 100 = 270
- Poached egg 70, with 1 slice chopped bacon 35 + juice = 205
- Egg McMuffin 70 + 35, English Muffin 110 + juice = 315
- I packet Oatmeal 130-160, Equal 0, 1/3 c soy milk 34, + juice = 264 - 294
- 1 cup Raisin Bran Crunch 190, 1/2 banana 40, 1/3 c soy milk 34 + juice = 364

Lunch
- 1 apple 80 1 slice cold turkey meat 25 1 slice cold ham meat 30 = 135

Afternoon snacks
> Rice cake 55 1/4 c refried beans 45 = 100
> Raw zucchini 22 1 carrot 30 = 52
> Celery stalk 7 stuffed with 1 Tblsp peanut butter 95 = 102
> Diet 7UP or Diet Pepsi 0

Dinner ideas
> Quesadilla 230 1/2 c refried beans 90 small salad 50 1 Tblsp lo fat dressing 35 = 405
> Burrito 330 rest the same = 505
> Caesar salad 2 c lettuce 20, 1 scallion 5, 1 mushroom 5, 1/2 tomato 15, 1/4 c croutons 35, lo fat dressing 70 = 150 + chicken breast 130 = 280
> 2 oz. Spam 170 1/2 baked yam 80 2 tsp Butter Buds 10 1 c broccoli 40 = 300
> Corn on cob 70 1 Tblsp I Can't Believe It's Not Butter 90, 1 c fresh green beans 31 chicken breast 130 = 321
> 6 raviolis 200 oil 50 or 1/4 c sauce 55 3 small meatballs 90 small salad 100 total = 445
> 2 oz grilled Kielbasa 180 roll 100 1/2 c baked beans 150 salad 100 = 580
> 4 oz grilled Salmon 250 grilled zucchini 22 salad 100 = 372

Treats
> 1/4 c Dreyers Sugar Free Triple Chocolate ice cream 100
> 1 glass of white wine 4 oz 100

1 oz booze 80 proof 100
12 oz can Olympia Lite 70

GOOD LUCK !!

KEEPING IT OFF

"Keep the faith"

Now as promised: How to keep that stuff off. Remember you lost the weight, you didn't just misplace it. So think of it as gone and you ain't gonna look for it !! Big words from a big mouth but fortunately I read the paper every day and I found an article: The title was something catchy like "Keeping the Weight Off Once You Lose It". Ready?

    1. Buy a small paperback calorie counter book.
    2. Get a little 3x5-spiral notebook and a pencil with an eraser
    3. Get a small hand calculator.
    4. Put it on the table where you eat your meals.
    5. Take it all with you if you go on a trip

That's the equipment you will need to write and record every single bite you eat each day.

Omigod! That is impossible. It's boring. It's a pain, etc.etc.etc. And it is all of that but still do it, and soon it will become routine. Honest. Trust me.

I thought I knew a lot about calories and what's good and what's bad. Was I ever wrong. I learned so much about calories, counting them and keeping track. I realized I was totally ignorant in this area. But I learned and have been doing it faithfully for over two years. And, the best part is, I still weigh what I weighed when I started keeping track. And I will never again, ever, be over what I consider a good weight for me.

Important! You have to have a goal. Weight maintenance for women is around 1200 calories per day. For men, it is about 1500. That varies depending on how much you burn if you exercise vigorously. At the beginning use the 1200 or 1500 number no matter how much you exercise so you'll get a feel of what you consume and what you burn.

At the beginning I was really obsessive about counting and writing. But as some time went by I calmed down a bit and realized how easy it was, and still is. I read calories on all labels of what I am buying. If it's too many calories for me to get a decent portion then I pass and choose something else. Fruits & vegetables & fresh meat demand that you use the book. My book also has some fast food places listed so you can go by their numbers. If you share Nachos Bell Grande (770) from Taco Bell, it's not too bad. One of my favorites from there is Mexican Pizza (570) so I really watch my diet the next day.

I write down the numbers for breakfast and lunch then do a sub total so I know what I have left for the day and can plan ahead. I like to have a drink before dinner (100) or a glass of wine (100) and I like a dish of Dreyers Sugar Free Triple Chocolate Ice Cream for dessert (1/2 cup 100). Add those to the sub total and I know what my dinner limitations are. It's not always easy but it works. Many evenings I have a big Caesar Salad sometimes with croutons and often with a grilled chicken breast (150 + 130 = 280). I have a bag of the grilled breasts in the freezer from Costco.

I started this regimen in March over two years ago. I weigh myself every Sunday or Monday and I'm right there. If I have a big week-end, I might be up a pound or two, so I cut back on the drink or ice cream. Or just eat less for a day or two - Bingo, I'm back where I belong. I find it absolutely amazing that this works and finally I am in control! What a wonderful feeling to know you can succeed!

Hint: Keep both a liquids measuring cup and a dry measuring cup very handy. I also have an old postage scales that I use to weigh and measure meat, for instance. As time has gone on I have developed a fairly good eye and any tool is a help, so I still measure my soy milk and cereal each time. As my grandma used to say, "better safe than sorry".

Something I learned through all this boringness that bears repeating, is a night on the town or a scrumptious lunch or a brief binge doesn't ruin everything. You just have to buckle down afterwards or else watch that scale climb! It is amazing how once you start and SEE the difference how easy it is to maintain. I'm on my 2nd little notebook and think those items will be a part of my life forever. And that's OK. If people tease you, it's because they are jealous. Don't succumb to their weaknesses!

I must mention some food things I learned along the way. Grapefruit juice is a delightful way to start the day. Unsweetened of course. There are only 100 calories in an 8 oz. glass whereas orange juice and others have more. And you need to cut where you can especially if your drink of juice in the morning is more important than anything else.

I have recently switched to soymilk. White Wave Silk has chocolate and vanilla flavored or regular. My choice is the regular.

It has only 100 calories to an 8 oz. glass so if you use a fourth or a third of a cup on your oatmeal or other cereals, it is only 25 or 34 calories. Sun Soy from the Morningstar Company in Dallas is also very good and only has 80 calories to a cup. Every bit counts and helps save up for something special for dinner. What I especially like about soy milk is its longevity. It lasts for 4 – 6 weeks and the date is clearly printed on each quart. But be careful because once lumps start forming it is not reliable any longer. Toss it.

And of course I use Equal instead of sugar. Zero calories. I have been told that Aspartame which is in Equal, Diet 7UP and other sugar free foods breaks down chemically into a substance like formaldehyde. You might want to verify that before you make any rash decisions.

Bread or toast can be a downfall. So look carefully at the wrappers and see what they say 1 or 2 slices are. Poached egg on toast can be 205 or more. Whereas poached egg and one slice of Oscar Meyer bacon is only 105! plus juice makes it only 205 for breakfast. Not bad. My favorite is hash browns from a new red potato previously boiled, diced and browned (104) in a non stick pan with a poached egg slathered over it, plus juice equals 274. And that is good. Oatmeal with soy, plus juice is 280. It all will work for you, too.

Lunch can be a problem. A lot of retirement homes and apartments have the big meal at noon & then a light dinner. Also a lot of seniors prefer to go out for a meal at lunch while it is daylight and not be out in the dark. These are choices we all make at one time or another and we calorie counters must make some decisions also. As for me, I will eat a light lunch out on occasion & try to count the calories. I just never have made that switch to a full time non-dinner in the evening. Someone asked me about eating alone. I said I read the paper at breakfast and have dinner with Larry King. For me a special occasion is a reason to dress up and have a scrumptious dinner with wine in a lovely restaurant. But that's just me and those times don't happen too often.

To make my normal dinners able to support some enriching, I am very careful about what I eat for lunch on a normal day to day basis. My favorite is a Fuji apple (80) and low fat sliced cold meat (protein). The turkey is 25 and the ham 30 so with the apple my lunch is about 135. Sometimes I eat it all at once & other times separated by an hour or so. And sometimes I have a rice cake (45) in the afternoon with a piece of meat or leftover low fat refried beans (45) or baked beans (75) sloshed all over it. There are always the old stand-bys for a snack: carrots, celery, zucchini etc. I also like Melba Round crackers (5 are 60) with any of the above. How about stuffed celery with the refried beans? Lots of potential for filling some empty and yearning tummies. Prunes are 30 each. Don't forget sometimes that a big drink of water will help. Also diet 7UP is 0 calories.

If I could do it at 70, you can do it at 55, 60, 65, 70, 75 or whenever. The longer you wait the more your skin is used to being stretched and the harder it is for your skin to pop back into some semblance of comfortable skin. Let's not kid ourselves. Our skin is old and is going to look old. We can hide it but we can't deny it. Grant Hughes, a retired Doctor and Psychiatrist, says, "Keep doing what you're doing, and you'll get what you're getting". And he's certainly right about our eating and other health habits.

There's one other thing to remember about dieting. It was always harder for me when I was working unless I took my lunch. Why do fellow employees think it is so great to bring a plateful of doughnuts or chocolate chip cookies for everyone as a treat? When you are at home each day you have so much more control. If you are restless and that empty stomach is gnawing at you, go for a walk. Sometimes I will go to the computer and play a bunch of games of solitaire. Or try reading a good book. Much as I love reading, it does not help when I am starving. I cannot have cookies or candy in the house. If I receive a gift I try to manage but end up bingeing just to get rid of the damn wonderful things! It's OK. You'll be like Scarlett O'Hara, and tomorrow is another day. Believe me, counting those calories does work.

Have you ever taken Citrimax? A couple of times a year I start being really hungry in the late afternoon or sometimes in the evening. When I know I'm into that eat-any-cost mode, I take 1 Citrimax half an hour before lunch and the same before dinner. In a few days I have cured the need and am back on track. I don't like to do it anymore than a few days, if at all possible. I haven't had any side effects but I don't want it to be a habit.

This is not a cookbook but some of this stuff I just have to share:

When cooking fish in the microwave, place it between 2 pieces of lettuce & cook as usual is what Dr. Hughes suggested.

When cooking vegetables in the microwave, sprinkle with a small amount of Equal. This has been suggested, but I haven't tried it. I steam my veggies.

An ear of corn on the cob left in its husk takes 4 minutes to cook on High in the microwave. It is so tender and juicy. Delicious. If you have two, they take 8 minutes and so on. They are very hot to hold and husk afterwards. Use a hot pad or glove, but be careful. Worth it!

My Dad used to consume only liquids one day a week. It worked for him to maintain the weight he wanted. I must mention that he didn't pig-out the rest of the week but he didn't deprive himself at meals either. Discipline is what it's all about. Remember that liquids fill you up at any time during the day.

Have you discovered spaghetti squash? Follow directions for baking, then fork it out in strands onto your plate & cover with ¼ c of Prego Roasted Garlic & Herb Pasta Sauce.

You will discover in your reading that peeled vegetables & fruits have less calories than with the peel left on. I choose to leave them on for the vitamins and roughage, but it is nice to know.

Microwave popcorn is another find worth remembering. However, read labels carefully.

A breakfast I have come to love frozen waffles heated in the toaster. There are many kinds to choose from, so read carefully. I find that one tablespoon of Log Cabin maple syrup (53) goes the distance for me. Naturally, lo-cal is less & you can slop more on.

You all know to eat slower so your tummy tells your brain, "Hey, I'm getting full" before you continue to stuff food in your face.

Weight Watchers suggests putting down your fork between bites and chew it all up before picking up the fork & continuing with the next bite. Makes sense to me if you can do it.

STAYING TRIM

"Hold back your shoulders and suck in your stomach"
"What goes around, comes around"

You must be active. I don't have a car anymore because I can walk to almost any place I want to go or take City transportation. Mostly, I walk and at a brisk pace a total of 18 - 20 blocks which takes 20 - 30 minutes. When I first started walking daily I would do it first thing in the morning before breakfast. I walked a mile plus every day. I always walk to the store with my handy cart (that is tall enough so it doesn't strain my back). My life is so full now and I have been walking for so many years, my menu is somewhat regimented and I find that I don't have to walk every day if my schedule is too full. However, when I am tired in the afternoon I find a brisk walk revitalizes me for the rest of the day.

    It was funny how habit controlled my walking for a year or two. I was used to walking that mile plus every morning, so after I moved I would get up and do it first thing before breakfast. Then when it was time to go to class I would take the bus. As I said it took me a couple years to figure out that I could actually walk downtown, save the bus fare, have extra time in the morning, and still get my exercise. And they say it's hard to teach an old dog new tricks!

My survey showed that 75% of the Seniors used walking as their form of exercise. It is always there and so easy to accomplish. All of them preferred walking to anything else.

Sometimes when walking you will get a funny feeling about someone you notice on the street. Don't hesitate to talk to a person of authority you hopefully will see. Often just the mere fact you talked to a cop will do the job. One day while walking home, I sensed that a weird man was possibly following me. I stopped a policeman and while chatting, turned around, pointed and the man disappeared. It worked and I had only asked the officer which direction the library was!

Remember, there is nothing like a brisk walk to make one feel better, to give one energy and an incentive to enjoy life. Be enthusiastic! Smile at the people you pass and say. "Hi! How are you?" Answer the Hi's you receive with a "I'm great! How are you?" Or "I'm terrific! How are you?" The point isn't to pick up strangers but to feel good and let it show. The responses will amaze you. I'll tell you an interesting thing that happened to me while walking a bit later.

I must mention Tai Chi Chih again. It really helped my balance and also gave my brain a rest. Now I have a video that I use when I want. You might investigate this discipline. It's fun, relaxing and invigorating at the same time. There are groups all over the country that teach and practice Tai Chi Chih faithfully. Recommended!

Some people love to exercise or lift minor weights. It does keep up your strength and is so good for you. The Y and other groups have many programs to offer. My survey showed that group exercise wasn't most Senior's exercise of choice. I think it is a matter of what you are used to doing. Investigate and try different programs. Swimming at the Y is wonderful. Often they have times or classes just for seniors so you're not out there competing with the slim, trim and so damn firm young 'uns. Do it.

Another thing we seniors tend to do is stumble, trip, and fall down. I did too much of that when I first moved up here. A leaf on the pavement, an acorn, a crack in the sidewalk all caused me to lose my balance and fall. I was lucky and only had skinned knees and arms and once a sprained wrist. What I started doing to correct this habit was to lift the front part of my feet a little bit more when I walked. It took some practice. Now when I stumble I know why and start walking smarter again. Also, learn to just drop when you fall. Don't put a hand out to catch yourself. Eventually you'll be sorry. Just practice walking differently and it should help. Hopefully, it will become the way you walk.

If you live in a complex that has several floors and one or two stairwells, you are so lucky. Walking up and down those stairs is one of the best exercises for your legs. My knees are not in the best of shape so I only walk down and do that quite often. Al used to go up and down all 12 flights by stairs whenever he went to the roof garden. He was thin and in great shape. He moved away but I miss his example.

Do you play tennis? Racquet ball? Golf (walking, not riding in a cart)? Some of the sports we love tend to be expensive so we substitute other things. But if you have access to these sports, be sure to keep them up. They are good for your mind as well as your body. Sports are also a wonderful way to make new friends. Organize a baseball team and games in your senior's neighborhood. Women can play as well and all mates should attend to cheer on the home team. Then have a barbecue.

A fun activity that you alone or with a partner can do is folk dancing. And ballroom dancing lessons are available in many communities. You just have to get up out of the chair and do something. Call the resources mentioned throughout the book. You can't lose.

Practice good posture. You can have a beautiful healthy body, but if you are all slouched with stomach sticking out and dragging your feet, you don't look or feel beautiful or handsome. I think posture is very important. I have been amazed at the people that have mentioned my posture to me. To some it was the first thing they noticed about me. That's nice and encouraged me. Try! Remember how we used to walk around with a book on our heads practicing for something. Well, this is what you were practicing for. Do it!

So those are some things on which we can all keep working.

HEALTH

"You can do anything if you just set your mind to it"

MEDICAL THOUGHTS

"Better safe than sorry"

It can be a scary process looking for the right medical help for yourself when you move to a new community. Here are some ways that have been helpful for me. 1) Before I moved I asked my doctor and dentist as well as local friends if they had any acquaintances in my new locality or recommendations. I got a few names and called them when I got here and proceeded from there. 2) Your medical insurer should be sending you a list of medical personnel on their list when you notify them of your address change. That helps! 3) If you live in an apartment complex or any kind of a closed community, ask around. I'm sure you will get many opinions! 4) And of course, there is always the phone book to find someone in your neighborhood 5) When you get a name, make a get-acquainted appointment And 6) Just because you try someone once doesn't mean you have to go to that person forever.

That awful "H" word comes to mind sometimes when I think of my general health. You all know it the word: Hemorrhoids. Or rhoids as I called it (them) in my piece titled "Hemorrhoids or Suicide". My first sentence started, "I think I made the wrong choice—". Rhoids are something that none of us wants to have a thing to do with and most people won't talk about it. It is misery with a capital "M". I had that lovely surgery when I was 60 and spent the first week afterwards lying in the Jacuzzi or the tub. It was awful and I swore I would never have that problem again.

Lotta good swearing did. When I was 70 I started noticing a bit of bright red blood in my stool. The bright red was good but it wouldn't go away in spite of all my efforts. 6 or 8 prunes a day, Metamucil, etc. So I visited a specialist and had a probing and photo shoot of the whole area (colonoscopy). I was clean and healthy. Hooray! But I kept bleeding and in pain from the inspection. Back I went and he told me (without an examination) to take more hot baths each day. Hell, I had been doing that for weeks and nothing worked. I was still very uncomfortable.

I happened to mention the problem to my chiropractor who then told me his own tale (tail) of woe. The upshot was that he referred me to a chiropractor, Steven Gardner, who specialized in rear ends! I visited this miracle man 8 times. He healed the 3 torn fissures from the inspection and used his magic instrument to annihilate the 3 little hemorrhoids that were growing in there. From the first treatment, I started feeling relief. I continued warm baths and caught up on my reading while in the tub. After 8 sessions, I was totally healed. And there was no agonizing pain. I couldn't believe the joy of relief I felt after all I had gone through before. If you ever have this problem, find a healing chiropractor and try it. It worked for me and I wish I had known about the possibility in the first place. I never would have had the initial surgery.

Since that experience I have recommended Dr. Gardner to another friend, Dorothy. She had put off surgery three times and about to finally succumb to a fourth scheduling. Instead she went to Dr. Gardner and came away cured after six visits. It cost her a total of $325 for absolute total relief from her hemorrhoids. A follow up visit after six months is requested by their office. I didn't do it because of transportation problems, but Dorothy is definitely planning to see him again. It is a wonderfully, unbelievable experience.

When I asked my hero chiropractor what to do to avoid further problems, he gave me a box of tea bags. I drank a cup each day (usually mixed in an Old-Fashion) before dinner. Then each morning, often before breakfast, I was relieved for the whole day. The tea is called Smooth Move and it is wonderful. Pam says that Swiss Kriss that is available at health food stores is also good. It is herbal leaves and you chomp down 1 or 2 teaspoons. Personally I like Old Fashions.

David, an R.N., told me that the skin on the small of our backs is the least sensitive part of our anatomy. I didn't believe him at the time but I do now. A friend, Jim, was sitting on the hearth of his fireplace one evening while chatting with friends and having a cocktail before dinner. He was very comfortable and feeling cozy warm, but not ever hot. However, when he undressed for bed that night he discovered that his back was burned and blistered. When he went to the doctor the next day, he was told he had second degree burns! Now that is scary! Jim hadn't felt a thing. Interesting knowledge to pass on to you.

Over twenty years ago I had the joints in my big toes replaced. They were totally ruined, probably from stumbling playing golf bare foot as a kid, and for a while there I could only walk in wooden soled shoes. It was awful. I found a wonderful podiatrist, Dr. Joe Errico, who performed the surgery and within a very short time I was wearing any shoes I chose. The joints cause me absolutely no problem and since they have lasted this long, I have been told they will probably last as long as I do. And that will be a long time indeed.

Various friends have had hip or knee replacements. I have heard only good reports from each of them. They are so happy to be active without pain again. Isn't it wonderful what can be done for us? If you have any of these problems, do see your doctor and a specialist. Get enough opinions to satisfy you. Take a list of questions along and get answers to each and every one.

Some people are very happy with various alternative forms of medicine and I say, investigate and try what you are comfortable doing. I subscribe to Dr. Andrew Weill's Newsletter and also UC Berkeley's medical letter. An excellent way to keep abreast of what is happening in all types of medicine, especially when you send for the year end index. There are many monthly publications out there. Try one and always get the free one first to see if it is for you.

How many of you see your dentist at least twice a year? I see the hygienist four times a year to have my teeth cleaned. I determined a long time ago that my teeth build up plaque faster than two times a year could handle. And don't you think it is a good investment to keep teeth and gums healthy so you don't have to get false teeth? Ask your dentist or hygienist what their opinion is. I recently bought a Braun Electric Toothbrush. It has a circular rotating brush/bristle. I have been told it will keep my gums strong and that's why I bought it. Maybe I can see the dentist only twice a year if this works as advertised.

Something I have noticed about many Seniors is their breath. It is often bad. It doesn't have to be. It could be a chemical imbalance in your system or you may have an unknown infection. Be sure to ask your dentist or hygienist for any suggestions to take care of this socially restrictive problem. I did, and got a tool that scrapes my tongue. There are various kinds of these tools. Plus brushing the tongue helps. Also, floss thoroughly frequently. Try gargling and brushing your teeth before you leave the house. And carry some breath mints in your pocket. You never know who is around the corner.

Another word about dentists and a wonderful invention. When I was about 60, I noticed that my teeth were starting to yellow. Uck! I didn't want them to be that bright sparkly white of a 15-year-old but I didn't want them that brownish yellow of an old, old person either. So I had them bleached. And I am so pleased. They gave me my fake set of teeth so I have a place to keep the fitted mouthpiece of my teeth that I wear when I renew the bleach job twice a year. You can buy the refresher cleaner from your dentist for self-application. You put the bleach into the mouthpiece and wear it overnight. Voila! Also, there are commercial adhesive bleaching tapes and other products that you can buy directly from the drugstore. I so recommend whitening your teeth. Frankly, they look awful when they turn yellow or brown and add years to your appearance. My friends that have used this procedure are extremely pleased and look terrific! So can you!.

I have a friend who is a nurse and mostly wears the white uniforms. I began to notice the contrast of color between her uniforms and her teeth. It was quite apparent. I agonized over how to mention it to her in the nicest way I could. I managed to do so one day when I talked about my bleach job. She then noticed the disparity herself for the first time and promptly had her teeth treated. She is extremely pleased and glad that I cared enough for her to mention this wonderful treatment. She just hadn't noticed the difference in colors.

Is there a need to mention having a physical once a year? I hope not. Be sure to make a list of your questions for the doctor so you don't get home and say, "Damn! I forgot to ask about all the belching I do." And mammograms & moles & warts & ingrown toenails, et al. You might think about taking your mate along so he/she can hear the answers. So often we slide over answers that our mate really should hear in totality.

If you are having trouble with your hearing, take the test and get a hearing aid. It is so annoying to your friends who care about you when you just miss out on things. Is it money or vanity that keeps people from getting one? A good friend of mine absolutely cannot hear out of one ear. So at movies, meals, walks, whatever, one has to be on the correct side or she misses everything. And then wonders later why she wasn't told something. I hope you are not this silly. Don't miss out. You are too smart to be so damn stubborn.

Several big macho men I know still seem to have that feeling of immortality, an "it can't happen to me" attitude. And how about the women who are just too busy to do the healthy thing? Get over it. All those things that your friends have or you have read about can happen to you. Naturally, your chances of avoidance are better if you take care of yourself. Like smoking that has reared its ugly self again. Emphysema, senior onset asthma and alcoholism, cancer or any of those illnesses or diseases you are encouraging. Yes, encouraging. Quit those damn cigarettes and cigars somehow. Watch when and how much you drink. Get help! You can do it!

Sleeping can be a big problem for some seniors. Frequently I go to bed dead tired and know I am going to fall asleep instantly. It seems to me that as soon as I get snug and comfy, my brain says, "At last. You turned off the TV. You closed the book. It's finally quiet in here and it is my turn". Does that happen to you? Ten minutes later I'm wide-awake.

I took a course, read a book, and also went to a counselor to learn about self-hypnosis. It is a fine solution to many of our sleep problems. I have a tape that I use occasionally and when it goes off after a while, I'm gone. Basically, 1) you lie on your back & take deep relaxing breaths, 2) concentrate on relaxing each part of your body starting with your toes and slowly work your way up, 3) Try to make your mind blank except for the relaxing thoughts. Normally you wake up when rested. Inquire about this by getting a book or seeing a professional therapist or hypnotist.

Another thing I try for getting to sleep is to close my eyes and stare at something and only think about that mark you are looking at. It does help to relax the brain. There are also tapes you can use. If you try this method make sure your tape deck has an automatic quiet turn-off. Otherwise, there's a loud click that wakes you right up or the radio comes on. Swell. There's always the old stand-by of counting sheep. You might try counting backwards from 100.

Something else that works if I wake up in the middle of my night or just absolutely can't drop off is to get up and play Solitaire on the computer. I play for maybe half an hour until I get droopy. It works and shuts off my brain. I wonder how much the handful of raisins that I eat at the same time helps. Sometimes I think it's the raisins, not the Solitaire!

One of the things to investigate if any noise bothers you is earplugs. There are all kinds out there and I have found that the only ones I can deal with, called Quiet Please, go way into your ear and have no sticking-out part to touch the sheet or pillow or your arm. If the plug touches something it is an annoying feeling and sound. Mine are white and you squeeze and roll them real tight and stick one in each ear. I pull my lobe down to get a better opening & shove it in. After the first night, they start fitting better. One end is for inside and the other is for outside and I couldn't tell them apart. So I take a Magic Marker and put a big black dot on the outside edge. Now I have no problem telling in from out. A pair usually lasts about a month or six weeks. I started wearing them so I couldn't hear snoring and now I wear them every night. Habit, I guess.

Apartments, condos, co-ops and big buildings often don't have the cross ventilation that you might be used to. I bought a ceiling fan for the bedroom and have it on 24/7. I love to feel a breeze on my face and this works perfectly. It is wonderful. I managed to put my bed next to the window and with the fan on all year 'round I am very happy.

And one more time I must mention the necessity of exercise, exercise, exercise. Walk as often as you can. That's why I like a City. It's too expensive to park so you walk. Or take a bus. Again, think about joining a gym or health club. Maybe you'll be lucky and your community will have an exercise room (with TV) as my building does. And of course, continue to participate in sports. Just get some sort of exercise every day!

MENTAL HEALTH

"It's not what I say, but what I mean"

"If you can't say something nice about a person, don't say anything at all"

There are two women I know who are so negative that I absolutely do not want to be around them if at all possible. I try always to be polite and not be rude. When I see them, I always greet them cordially and keep right on walking. If they persist in conversation, I will be polite and then move on as soon as possible. Negativity is too debilitating and we often don't have that extra energy to expend either during a conversation or afterwards when we are kicking ourselves for participating. Just don't get involved.

There are always people out there who will try to suck you dry. Don't let them. Easy for me to say but it is true. Been there, done that. You just have to practice and remember how important you are! And - more immediately - No one is going to do it for you.

I took a class called "It's the Thought that Counts" at OASIS all about our mental health. There were excellent points that I want to share with you about Twisted Thinking from Health Stages 2001, published by The OASIS Institute.

1. All-or-Nothing Thinking. You make one mistake on a project and decide the whole thing is hopeless. Or if your husband reprimands you, you think he doesn't love you.
2. Labeling. You make a mistake and think you're a jerk or you have an argument with a friend and you think, "I'm hard to get along with".
3. Over-generalization. Tip-off words, "always" and "never". Examples: "I'm always so clumsy." or "I'll never get it right."
4. Mental Filtering. In situations that involve both positive and negative elements, you dwell on the negative. You tend to filter out the good comments and concentrate on the bad.
5. Discounting the Positive. Tip-off phrases, "Anyone could do that" and "It isn't good enough". When you're praised or do something really commendable, you say those things to yourself.
6. Jumping to Conclusions. You assume the worst based on no evidence.
7. Magnification. You exaggerate the importance of problems, shortcomings and minor annoyances.
8. Emotional Reasoning. You mistake your emotions for reality. "I feel lonely, therefore I must be bad company".
9. "Should" and "Shouldn't" Statements. You play a game well but make one mistake and feel I shouldn't have done that. I'm not very good. Other key words are "must", "ought to", "have to".

10. Personalizing the Blame. When your grown child makes a mistake, you think, "I must have been a bad mother" or "I didn't set a good example".

I listed all these because I wanted you to see how easy it is to sink into blue funks and end up with a case of depression. Sometimes it only takes becoming aware of an idea to help one along but if you can't handle some of these symptoms, seek counseling. There are a lot of wonderful, competent and kind helpers out there. And because there are so many of us Seniors these days, there is a vast new market developing for geriatrics. Check out The Aging Counsel or something similar in your community. They can direct you to the right people. Specialists. Take advantage and use all of the opportunities available to you. Life is too short. "Remember the mustard seed"

Sometimes if we are depressed, it behooves us to sit back and say, "What happened? What am I feeling? Why? What did I do? What can I do about it?" If you are at all intuitive and honest with yourself, you can often figure out and solve some of your own problems. However, if it continues, see a counselor.

Do you ever listen to the radio? The stations that play music from your generation are wonderful to listen to when you need some cheerful distractions. When Dick Tench comes up once a week for cocktail hour we listen to Frank Sinatra and sing the old songs. Sometimes I play tapes from World War 2 for him. We know most of the words and sing along. Once in a while those old songs can help depression or a blue funk. You don't have to have company to play nostalgic and happy music. Just enjoy it for you.

Edna was telling me of a friend of hers who doesn't like to give her age. She has found that as soon as she says how old she is, she is immediately categorized in that other person's mind. Much like the police sometimes profiles people. I found this an interesting idea. It is something to think about. My own experience has been that usually when I give my age I am making a point and gaining a bit of respect from younger people. Tracy used to say to me, "just wait until you're my age". And my grandmother said, "just wait until you're 62". Well, I waited and got there and found I was still the same person. I think that you don't make any points being younger than the other person, but it's definitely more fun to be considered wise by some of those young smart asses out there!

Don't we all wonder at some time what makes us tick? What keeps us going? How do we handle adversity? For some it is God and for others it is their inner strength. That inner grit comes from God for some people. My Dad used to say, "Keep the faith" and I cherished him for reminding me of that in his letters along with his other homily, DLTBGYD. It is important for us Seniors to have a base of spirituality in our lives. For some it has been a formalized religion that we practiced since our childhood. For others it is a re-birth that we gained along the way. And for some people, it is just something we know we have inside of us that gives us courage, strength and love. Whatever you have, be grateful and keep practicing what is best for you.

UNKIND PEOPLE

"Rise above it. Don't lower yourself to their level"

The first time I heard that phrase, I was probably seven years old. I came crying home because my best friend who lived across the street, Pat, had gotten mad at me and threw me out her back door. My Mom comforted me and listened to all that I was going to do to get even with that brat. After letting me spout off for a few minutes, she said, "Don't lower yourself to her level. Rise above it." As similar occasions rose again off and on over the years, Mom always came through with those words. It usually settled me down and you can see I never forgot.

There have been many times in my life when I called that philosophy to mind and handled my difficulties in a manner that stood me in good stead. I don't know what the effect was on the other person when I didn't respond as was expected, but I know how much better and comfortable I felt with myself. It was gratifying knowing that I didn't have to be a mean & vicious person just because my "opponent" was. Pat stopped throwing me out her back door long ago but other people have tried similar tactics and they just don't work if you don't let them. I must share with you that Pat and I correspond on a regular basis. We both treasure and laugh over all those long ago memories.

Sometimes while voluntarily serving on committees, circumstances and impromptu speeches can become a major pain. Keep your dignity and do what you signed up for. It's the other person's problem, not yours. So don't take those things personally, just rise above it and go about your business. I have friends who were so distressed by certain turns of events that they didn't know what to do and ended up walking out. What a shame. My reply usually is: Is it worth it? Are you injuring your health? Will the whole thing fall apart if you quit? Watch out for yourself, no one else is. Right? Right!

Living in a large complex of any kind is an experience that is unique to most living arrangements. Some of the tenants stick totally to themselves while others are outgoing and eager to make new friends. Of course there are cliques that may or may not want you to join. Does this sound like junior high or high school? Sometimes it works best to be on the fringe of many groups rather than in the inner circle of only one. You must do what is most comfortable for you. My advice is to take your time.

There are horror stories galore about betrayals, gossips and just plain troublemakers. There seems to be no way to avoid these circumstances because newcomers just don't know what makes the others tick. My only advice is to be kind, be tactful and be honest without hurting anyone's feelings. Good advice is don't discuss your personal problems or difficulties in front of others. With a good friend, Yes, but with the rest of the tribe, definitely, No. After five years in this building I still find myself being surprised by some of tenants. You all know this but once in a while it bears hearing again. Rise above it. Turn the other cheek.

A word I have been trying to delete from my vocabulary is "hate". It is such an inflammatory word and the ultimate in disliking a person or a thing. What I have been doing for the past few years is trying only to hate what the person does, not the person.

Often people don't hear it that way but you at least know what you said. Try. The next step for me is to eliminate the word entirely, but it's hard. It just slips out sometimes.

Sometimes at our age it's difficult to realize that this petty garbage still goes on, but it does. It especially hurts when after a lengthy friendship, you feel stabbed in the back. One thing I learned is that those people often don't have a lot in their lives in the way of activities, interests, and various types of friends so they lash out at the known. And sometimes those people are just jealous. Go on about your business. Remember all the wonderful other friends and acquaintances that you have. You are a winner and don't let anyone tell you differently. Consider the source. Don't let the bastards get you down!

Once again, it's DLTBGYD.

All of that is very good advice, but what do you do if you are dealing with a control freak that happens to be a parent. It happens. Robin, in her 50's, lost her job that she had for 16 years, and her Mother stepped in to help her financially as Robin was going through her savings at a rapid rate. Mom is almost 80 and had just taken over Robin's life. She seemed to be always telling her what to do and yelling and screaming at her over everything. Robin is now getting counseling and desperately trying to find a new job. She has walked out of Mom's house and is living in her old apartment and they aren't speaking. Isn't that sad?.

I think there is a large fear factor going on here with Mom. I think she thinks, "What will Robin do if something happens to me? What if something happens to Robin, what will I do?" Because Robin chose to get counseling, I am sure there will be an understanding between the two down the line. I bring this all up to remind us, if we are mean to our children, or if they are mean to us, we have to work it out. Take pride out of it and try for a solution of better communication. It is everybody's fault. Not just one persons.

I love this quote from Alice Roosevelt Longworth. As the honored guest at a formal dinner, Mrs. Longworth was asked whom she would like seated next to her. She replied, "Someone who doesn't have anything nice to say about anyone, seat her/him next to me".

> There's so much good in the worst of us,
> And there's so much bad in the best of us,
> It hardly behooves any of us,
> To talk about the rest of us !

And I love this one –
> Great minds discuss ideas.
> Average minds discuss events.
> Small minds discuss people!

CHANGES OR HOW I HAVE CHANGED

"It ain't over 'til it's over"

When I looked in the mirror and noticed that my mouth wasn't gaping open as I put on my eyeliner and mascara, I was stunned. There I was in my 74th year and I had been wearing eyeliner & mascara for about 55 years and all those times my mouth automatically fell open. It was explained to me when I first noticed the phenomenon that it was a reflex, an automatic reaction, and totally uncontrollable. I tried but it continued to hang open until this year. What happened? How come now??

This section is to help you become aware of things that are going on, or not going on, in your life today. Things to think about and maybe realize your own changes. Some are good, healthy, and helpful. If you think about it and find some nasty ones, get rid of them. Enjoy the changes because there are sure to be more!

The word "interesting" is an interesting word. The dictionary defines it as, "exciting curiosity or attention". I have found that "interesting" is often used because the user can't think of another word that serves the same purpose. It also allows a person to tell a small fib, such as, "your outfit is interesting" or "that was an interesting statement".

Interestingly, it makes me laugh!

Those questions continued to bother me and as the days, weeks went on I realized that there have been other changes that also amaze me. As if applying make-up had loosened the rules somehow. This learning has nothing to do with physical ailments like arthritis. This is just about observations, enlightenment and once in a while some effort on my part.

When I first began using make-up, the lipstick was applied to only the lips and never, ever over those boundaries. Now the lips themselves are narrower (years of gritting teeth, my theory) but the edges aren't so clearly defined! So, one can break out of the narrowness and end up with a nice full lower lip that actually looks OK!

Of course there are all those gravity jokes about bust lines and bellies, but what happened to my butt? It is gone, just plain gone. That nice rear end that was attractive and pattable is just gone. Where? Slacks don't look the same anymore. What happened?

And the damn brassieres are no longer possible to fasten in the back. I have tried and tried and now just put them on inside out and backwards and fasten them in the front. It all seems so strange but I learned and I changed.

The most exciting thing I have learned is that there are pockets in my bladder. I didn't know that. Has my bladder changed too? Older people always complain about how often they have to go to the toilet and I had those same thoughts. However, I learned that if I just sit there an extra 10 or 20 seconds I will urinate some more. And sometimes sit a little longer still and there will be more. And I have changed and accepted this extraordinary learning experience. I think men knew this all along.

I have been living alone for eight years now and have learned that I have value as a woman. Not that I don't have value as a Mom, or didn't have value as a wife. But now I am all by myself and have value as a single, intelligent, independent, and competent woman. It is a glorious feeling that I treasure. I look in the mirror, and yes it's still me, but better. How come I never felt that way when I was happily married?

For this next one I am grateful that my Grandma and my Mom are no longer around to read this next change. I have decided that housekeeping is the least important thing in my life! Wow! It took courage to say that. What I have substituted for cleaning is orderliness, and it works! I might vacuum once a month. And yes, the bathroom gets cleaned a little more often than that, but not much. And sheets on the bed are supposed to be changed every week. Why? I sleep alone and shower & shampoo twice a week so I don't think the sheets are a festering dirt pile. I'm content. Comfortable changes!

A necessary change that has occurred because of a faulty senior memory and I once again am grateful that I am able to change and accept it and even brag about it. I mean, why not? When out of the blue sky I think of something to do, buy, wear, say, write I immediately write it down. No more, "damn, I forgot what I wanted to remember". Smart, huh?

Why is it that men who like a woman and date her, seem to think that they have to call her all the time? I can remember that was important in high school probably because both girls and boys were so insecure socially, that they kept in constant contact. Apparently, they didn't want anyone else near their territory. But now, why do those old men do that? I can only guess, but I think most single, senior men are lonely. And of course, some women are also, but many I know don't want the bother unless it's important. Makes sense to me. What a wonderful change. Of course, different strokes for different folks makes sense also.

Call me naïve, but I wasn't fully aware of the vast difference between the phrases "I love you " and "I'm in love with you". I have learned that I love lots of people (men and women) but I can truly only be in love with one. Have to be careful what we say.

Another change I have discovered is that there are different ways to step on and off curbs to make it easier on your back. When you approach a curb from the street, lift one leg up and place it just barely on the sidewalk curb and then bring your total weight up to rest on that one leg, and then bring your other foot/leg up to stride on your way. And do the same thing stepping off a curb. Put one foot down right at the edge, transfer your total weight to that leg and only then, stride off. It takes some practice but worth it.

Some words about the variety of friends that are available. There are all colors, shapes, sizes, religions, etc. with whom one can become friends, buddies, etc. I have always prided myself on having the ability to be open, non-judgmental, unbiased, non-prejudiced and all those other words. But what I discovered in my 70's that a difference in the ages of my friends open whole new vistas for each of us. This started a few years ago but at the moment I am 74, my best female friends are 65, 42, and 29! Isn't that fabulous? They ask & respect my ideas and opinions and I treasure their thoughts and feelings!

And last but far from least: The day came when I couldn't bend my legs enough to pull on my stockings, socks or knee highs. I just couldn't reach my feet. A dilemma, for sure. And since I walk all the time & get plenty of exercise, or so I thought, I had to change my thinking . So I learned some exercises to strengthen my back that I could do each morning before I got out of bed! The day begins when I get out of bed and I have already accomplished a goal. No more problems with the stockings!

These changes at my age have been a wonderful experience and I am grateful. I have older friends who brag, "I don't want to learn anything new and I'm not about to change. I got this far and that's that". Isn't that sad? I'm delighted I am still young and still learning! Interesting!

SEX

LOOKING FORWARD TO SEX

"It's not whether you win or lose, but how you play the game"

"Don't hide your light under a basket"

"Don't kiss on the first date"

Life changes for some people now, but not necessarily you. For most people your life will go on as you have been living it for the past few years. If sex was a part of your life yesterday it will be tomorrow. In talking to some retired couples about the subject I found the men tended to exaggerate (according to their wives) while the women were more conservative. Apparently, attitude for some individuals hasn't changed and their personalities and opinions are the same about some subjects as they were 30 years ago.

Some men use Viagra, Cialis or Levitra and don't want to admit it (according to their wives) and others couldn't say enough good things about it. Any man, any age (40 – 80) with E.D. should check with his Doctor about using one of these medications. (More about Viagara later.) Practically all were willing to admit a lubricant is used. My happiest retired married friends are the ones who love and enjoy their mates in most aspects of their total lives. I feel so sorry for friends who feel they are just putting in their time until they die. Isn't that sad? It is their choice.

For single Seniors going out on a "date" the first time is almost a traumatic experience. They haven't been with anyone new in ever so many years and it is certainly a different event, no denying that. But it happens and sometimes turns out wonderfully and most times it is only an evening out. I don't like using the word "only" because it is exactly that but actually a lot more. You have broken the mold and are trying new things. Go for it, keep trying.

My neighbor, Mary, met Wayne at a Senior Center and they dated for a couple of years. I remember how filled with trepidation she was at first and nervous and worried and fretful. She had been a widow for over a year and hadn't dated for over 40 years. I kept saying, "It's OK. Dick would be happy for you." I think she needed all the reassurance she could get. Now Mary and Wayne are very happily married. Wayne still lives in his house and Mary still lives in hers. They sleep over and have meals together, travel together, and have loads of fun together but still are independent. It's an unusual way, but it works for them. Actually, it sounds quite satisfactory for many people.

Single women are so free from the hang-ups of past generations and it seems foolish to me not to take advantage of that freedom. Often when a man asks me out, I let him pay the first time to see what direction it seems to be going and what his motives are. If I want to continue the "dating" routine, I often will say, "Next time let's each pay our own way". That way I feel absolutely free of any obligation, (which is important to a lot of people) plus I can suggest dates on other occasions. But hey, if the other person wants to treat for a special occasion, why not? Also, sometimes the guy just wants to pay because it has always been that way, and if I like him and am interested, then I let him. I love the freedom of choice. (Is it a date if you both pay your own way?)

It has been my experience that men will somehow let you know if they are interested in sex and what they eventually hope to achieve. If you aren't interested, say so. If that's the end of it, so be it. If not, you have a new friend with whom to enjoy parts of your life.

But be honest, as the truth will come out sooner or later. Better sooner. Life is too short. Let him continue with his search and you be yourself. You never know. Remember what they say about women changing their minds. Some men really get into the subject of sex and want to discuss all kinds of interesting aspects of it. I was somewhat taken aback the first time that happened, but now it's old hat and I just say, "I don't think so. I'm really not interested in talking about that". One man I see every once in a while says, "Oh that's right. You're not interested in sex." And I don't bother to correct him.

My survey revealed lots of interesting information. When I asked about sex for Seniors, some said they aren't interested anymore or just take care of it themselves and don't sweat any relationships. That seemed like a reasonable grown up answer. Also, from the survey, married couples have cut back a bit on the frequency but still have the desires and resulting pleasures with their mates. As I said not much changes those first several years.

Fran and Lou mentioned to me once that they continued to use condoms after 50 years of marriage even when they were in their 70's. It gave Lou more staying power and therefore, was more enjoyable for Fran. An interesting item to pass on to you. Wouldn't it have been nice if Viagara had been around when they were alive.

Some more survey stuff. Most of the people who are in warm, loving relationships now are very pleased and content. It seems the ones who have had those in the past miss them the most and continue to hope that something will turn up. One question in the questionnaire is "Have you found a new sex partner?" My favorite answer was from a man who said, "Not yet".

The Seniors that have found new companions because of death or divorce all seemed so surprised that it (love) could ever happen to them again. They were thrilled and couldn't say enough wonderful things about their good luck and happiness. Isn't that encouraging?

The other side of the coin was a total lack of interest in finding a new companion. Many mentioned what a bother or complication another person could be. Others weren't willing to change anything in their lives to adapt to the presence of another person. I wondered if these people had always been that way. Or maybe life was so perfect they can't imagine anything any better. Whatever is right for you.

The main message from the survey seemed to me to be: "Life is good. I'm happy with my life. Something would have to be almost perfect or really special for me to change my life style".

Many of the women in the survey who are single now are quite happy in their situations. They have friends of both sexes that they enjoy as companions. What I found the women seem to miss is cuddling, holding hands at times, and gentle kisses.

They want the warmth but not the responsibility. Many were quite frank about not getting involved with men in a sexual way at this time in their lives.

In the old days, all girls were ga-ga over those tall handsome guys. And the guys were absolutely bug-eyed over big breasts and a nice ass (t & a). Are those values shallow or what? It seems to me that the studs & the beauties are mostly concerned with their own shallow needs. They truly are used to having everyone bow to their whims and some of them actually don't know how to love & cherish someone else. So folks, if you are thinking of dating, broaden your scope. Check out the other types. They are the nicest, and often the best, you'll ever meet. They will be grateful and care about you and cherish your friendship. Test the waters, you'll see.

The subject of very fat people has come up. Most lean people can't imagine having sex with a huge fat person. The question from women is, "Can it even be done in the normal (missionary) position?" Someone said it was impossible because if you are leaned on, you can't breathe and the close genital contact that is necessary for orgasm doesn't happen because that big belly gets in the way. Of course the women on top works well for orgasm for some couples but leg cramps sometimes happen. I don't think any of us are quite as athletic as we used to be. Men say about having sex with a fat lady, "please, I can't even imagine it". So there you are. Go on a workable diet if you want a new sex partner or if you want to renew that wonderful relationship you used to have.

I believe it is extremely important that we keep in mind the need for blood tests. There are too many serious things, HIV and AIDS, going around plus a resurgence of more minor problems like genital warts or even syphilis and gonorrhea. It's scary. And getting to this age without personally encountering any of it, I wouldn't want to wake up one day and find out I have HIV because I was stupid. So get the blood test to reassure a partner and make sure the other person gets one, too. It has been suggested that if you go to a free clinic, that you go together and totally share the results. Call the clinic beforehand to find out any details you may need to know. For instance, the length of abstinence since the last sexual encounter, if there is a fasting period before the blood test, etc. If you are having a physical, be sure to ask that they include the test from your personal blood sample and ask for a copy of the results. One woman friend told me she had three tests last year! I was amazed, but good for her and her partners. "Better safe than sorry"

I had a very interesting experience with a man I met, while walking down the street.

We had passed and I said, "Hi! How are you?" He replied, "Hi. I'm great. How are you?" I replied, "I'm terrific" and kept right on walking as he did. After a few steps I looked back and he did too, at the same moment. I quickly turned back and walked a few more steps and turned around again and there he was, also turning around. On the third turn-around he unlocked a door, waved and went inside. I kept on walking home.

The next day on my way to OASIS, I walked past the door he had entered which turned out to be his office door, and thought "what the hell" and went inside. He greeted me and told me he recognized me from the day before. I shook his hand and introduced myself. He told me his name was Michael and we exchanged business cards. And then we started going out. Not very often but enough to know that this could be interesting.

I told him my circumstances and asked about his. We never discussed in detail the age difference. He was obviously younger than I was and didn't seem to mind. Thank goodness! Eventually, I was curious about his recent sexual encounters. He had been with three different women in the past seven months. Michael probably regretted telling me, but I appreciated the honesty of his reply and told him there could be no sexual contact until he had a blood test. That changed things considerably. I'll never positively know the real reason for his delay in getting one, but he claimed to want to wait for his new job health insurance to kick in. I felt $20 at the health clinic wasn't a financial burden. But he clung to his idea and I clung to my demand. After a few months it ended. I saw him again on the street one day and asked if he had ever gotten the blood test. He said, "Yes. It was negative as I told you it would be". I laughed and said, "Sure".

This seems like a good place to share a joke. From a woman's point of view, a man who says he is fiscally conservative and socially liberal is a cheapskate who sleeps around.

The experience with Michael was delightful, innocent and fun while it lasted and I don't regret it or the outcome. What it did for me was immeasurable. I was really lacking in self-esteem and confidence in myself as a woman when we passed on the street that day. Michael gave it all back to me and then some. Since then I have gone out on a friendship basis with two different guys and have just met two more men that I see on occasion. I really feel good about myself in ever so many ways. So, thanks, Michael!

If you find a friend in a married man or woman, it can be a ticklish situation until you both make your positions and goals clear. Remember, there is an older mate at home for the other person and maybe even for you. Is it fair to get romantically involved at this late date? I don't think so, but you have to play by your own needs. A married friend of the opposite sex can be a delightful experience and one with whom you can share many good hours in conversation. After all, he or she, knows the ropes and can be a great source of comfort or share in your joy, whichever the case may be. Just be kind and careful. If you have a great marriage, don't blow it over this.

A lot of single women I know say they absolutely will not start a sexual relationship at this age. After much prodding I usually learn that they don't want anyone to see them bare. That is so understandable. Hey, men often feel the same way. You might remember that when he or she remove their glasses, they probably can't see too well anyway! I suggest candlelight and/or a dim hall light, a mute television emits a nice gentle glow, getting into bed with a nightie or pajamas on keeps everyone covered. You both will be comfortable that way at first and as your experience progresses, the clothing will probably come off. If it doesn't, it doesn't matter. This is your relationship and you both have to feel at ease to enjoy each other fully. And hey, isn't that what this is all about? You can always do it fully clothed in the car in a darkened garage!

So much about sex is not about the body. It's usually about the heart and the mind. The comfort level between two people is what is important and what we all seek. If guilt, shame, or one's inhibitions are uppermost in the mind, nothing beautiful can happen. The same is true if one is overly concerned about his/her appearance. It's important to talk to the other person about all aspects of what is happening. Better late than never. Work those things out and be free. There is a lot on the Internet that can be ever so helpful, and it's not porn.

I mentioned Viagara in passing at the beginning of this chapter and now I will elaborate a bit. One day I received a call from a lady who had heard about my forthcoming book from a friend and wanted to know if we could meet for lunch and talk about some things. I said I would, and we did. The lady, only known to me as Clara, told me this story. Once she started sharing her story she couldn't stop. She wants the world (especially readers) to know how great "retired sex" can be. Here's her tale (tail).

When in her early 70's, Clara met Ned, the same age, at a book club group to which they both belonged. No bells rang, just talking in the group and going their separate ways. One time Ned asked Clara to lunch, and it went on to become a weekly ritual. After a couple of months or so, Ned gave Clara a peck on the cheek to say good-bye. The next week she returned the gesture. The next week it was a mutual peck on the mouth.

The casual kisses continued for several more weeks. Clara was reluctant at first but it was so casual and friendly that she saw no cause for concern.. The conversations at lunch covered a little more of their personal backgrounds as the weeks went on. They were both divorced and neither of them had been involved with anyone for a few years. When Clara invited Ned to dinner at her place, more kissing ensued, but no aggressive action was initiated. However, the kissing was different this time. Slow and tempting, soft and gentle, teasing and suggestive is the way Clara described it. And the flame started smoldering. Clara thinks it was the romantic kissing that got them on track.

There wasn't any deep tongue stuff. Just those soft, sexy breathy kisses. When they had dinner at his place the following week with those same kisses, it all happened and the fire began.

Clara says their sex became the best sex she has ever, ever had. Multiple orgasms, the whole nine yards. Ned had gotten a prescription for Viagara (just in case, he told her) and it apparently is the wonder drug as advertised. Clara got this Cheshire Cat grin on her face when discussing their sex. I was amazed at her frankness but she just bubbled about the whole experience. Ned had easily found Clara's elusive clitoris and has given her "waves of ecstasy". That's the phrase she used, "waves of ecstasy". She had never had multiple orgasms and apparently these were beyond her control. Like 10 or 15 in an evening. I was impressed. Clara said the only down side to all this was the exhaustion that followed the next day, but she didn't care. It was worth it.

I would like to have interviewed Ned, but never did meet him. Clara was so impressed with his knowledge of the female body and his skill in using that information. She said he learned some of it from an acquaintance of several years back and has enhanced that with information from the Internet. He had been concerned about Erectile Dysfunction and found lots of useful explanations and help on his computer. Good deal, people!!

Ned's experience with Viagraa was a bit different. He only had one orgasm during each of their evenings together but could be erect at a moment's notice from the Viagara for a couple more hours of fun and games and Clara's pleasure. She said Ned never complained and was thrilled she was so happy. Quite an ego trip, I would guess.

What Clara also said is that Viagara totally got her off the hook for any responsibility for Ned's erections. She thinks that women just get fed up with having to get a man ready and then keep him erect. She claimed she used to do all the work, and for what? She said she just didn't want to have to help and feel responsible for a man's virility anymore, and now she doesn't. I think she makes a very good point. I wonder if that is why so many older, single women aren't interested in sex anymore. Maybe it became a drag.

I have wondered if Bill Steere, retired President of Pfizer, and his associates had any idea what a fantastic thing they were doing for the women of the world when they gave men Viagara. I bet they know now though!

Clara and I spent several hours talking and I learned so much. Ned takes the pill, has a wonderful time and Clara gets more pleasure than she ever had and knows it is going to happen every time because of that wonderful little pill! Her formula for successful sex and romance is: Ned's Viagara + her 2 drinks = perfect sex. When they sit together on the couch to watch TV, the closeness often prompts action. She keeps an afghan on the couch for convenience. It often ended up as cover for the rug and with the soft light from the TV or the fireplace they have a fine time. And in their 70's, too. I never saw Clara again as she has moved away, but I thank her for sharing her experiences with me, and you.

So Gals and Guys. If you have a hot body and meet someone whom you like, give yourself a chance. Don't be too afraid. Go slow. Take it easy. Don't scare the other person away by being overly aggressive. Give everyone a chance to be comfortable. You may be as totally surprised as Clara was. Actually,

Clara was as overwhelmed as Ned was. He had never made a woman so happy and she was ecstatic. Something Clara mentioned that made sense to me because we are older and often are a bit more inhibited and shy than we need to be, is having a drink. That's why Clara usually had a couple drinks before dinner. Ned might have had a half a drink only, because alcohol and Viagara don't mix.

Clara happily talked about that time in her life and how lucky she was to have met Ned. They continued their relationship for many months but other interests caused them to take different paths, and so they had parted. Apparently, it was never going to be a marriage and so no one was hurt when it ended. Neither regretted one moment of their time together. I believe this also points out that sex is still wonderful but as a Senior there are other bridges still to cross and life goes on. I wonder if they will ever rendezvous?

Gay men of all ages are great friends for women of all ages. I met a nice man, whom I will call George, shortly after I moved and settled into my apartment. He had recently moved into a neighboring building and was in a couple of groups at OASIS that I had joined. We liked each other instantly and had a couple of dates and discovered even more common interests. At the close of the third date, George leaned in and kissed me goodnight. After I closed the door I pondered over this and realized I didn't want a kissing kind of a relationship with George at this time in my life.

On our next date, George said he had to talk to me about something. And I thought this might be the perfect opportunity for me to share my negative feelings about our growing relationship. So in a quiet restaurant George talked about his past and how he couldn't be too serious with me and finally said. "I'm gay". I was so happy to hear those words because it totally let me off the hook, and I blurted out, "That's wonderful! I'm so glad!"

George and I have continued our best-friend relationship for many years. I wasn't committed to being anyone's exclusive property and I was able to see other men as the occasions arose. George is still one of the most interesting and intelligent men I have ever met and I am so grateful for our friendship.

So much for the exciting chapter on sex for retirees. There are almost as many options for retirees as there are people retired. Take your time and give a little, be kind, and enjoy yourself. Let life happen for you and to you. You never know. Just because we're older, doesn't mean we're dead.

A favorite and unforgettable quote of a friend mine is, "I hope the last person who touches me is not the mortician".

CONCLUSION
"All's well that ends well"

CONCLUSION

I hope you have enjoyed reading this book as much as I enjoyed writing it. If you learned one or two things you are that much ahead. I learned lots from the questionnaires and am delighted with the responses.

When you decide to retire, choosing a location is a huge step. There are so many options and it seems it is up to you to choose only one. Not necessarily. Do one for a while and then change if you are discontent or restless. Remember we are only here once so "enjoy all the stops along the way".

The next big step of course is finding living accommodations and settling in. There is a lot to take into consideration and I hope I helped you with some thoughts. It's so important that we remember the needs of our mates and partners. Making friends and getting involved in your new community is a challenge that most of us haven't given much thought to until this happened, unless we were transferred a lot in our jobs. But this is different; this can be permanent if you want it to be.

I hope I didn't ruffle too many feathers in my comments about our Senior appearance. It continues to amaze me what unattractive things I see people doing and wearing each day. It's no wonder they are unhappy and depressed.

The eating plans are guaranteed to take off that excess weight if you stick to it. And as Dr. Irish says, "exercise, exercise,

exercise". And I know you can keep the weight off if you start counting calories religiously every single bite you take and write it down. Do it.

This isn't a medical or psychological treatise and I tried to stay away from getting in too deep in some of those categories. But do watch out for unkind and/or negative people. They can do more to ruin your day, your week, and your life than anything I know. They just suck that energy right out of you. Don't play their game. Be yourself and remember "You catch more flies with honey than you do with vinegar". Thanks, Grandma!

Sex. Be yourself. Don't be afraid to learn and then practice new things. You can enjoy it all if you let loose a little bit. I believe as we get older, we don't really change, we just become more of what we were and are. You can become more of the negative, narrow minded you, or you can become the happy, open minded, willing to grow and learn person that is truly inside of you! Do it! Good luck!

"Continue doing what you are doing, and you will get what you are getting"

ADDAGES, APHORISMS & BON MOTS

DLTBGYD Don't Let The Bastards Get You Down

It's not whether you win or lose but how you play the game

What goes around, comes around

There's more than one way to skin a cat

You're only as young (or Old) as you think

If you can't say something nice about someone, don't say anything at all

Two heads are better than one

All's well that ends well

To thine own self be true

Keep doing what you're doing then you'll get what you're getting

The early bird catches the worm

Character is a victory, not a gift

Do unto others as you would have them do unto you

A job worth doing is a job worth doing well

If you start something, finish it

Time and tide wait for no man

If you would only act as nice as you look

Pretty is as pretty does

Rise above it. Don't stoop to their level

Give in on the little things. Never give in on the big things

It's not what I say, but what I mean

You catch more flies with honey than with vinegar

You can do anything if you just set your mind to it

Don't wear stripes and plaids together

Always wear clean underwear in case you are in an accident

Don't you want to belong to the Clean Plate Club?

Let the chips fall where they may

If you don't try it, you'll never know if you can do it or not

A stitch in time saves nine

It's better to tell the truth and be punished than to tell a lie

Hold back your shoulders and hold in your stomach

An apple a day keeps the doctor away

Honesty is the best policy

Two's company, three's a crowd

If a man's socks are neat & pulled up, then he is a gentleman

A watched pot never boils

Too many cooks spoil the soup

What's done is done

Better safe than sorry

Always keep both feet on the ground

Squeaky hair is clean hair

Drive defensively

Keep the faith

Remember the mustard seed

Don't kiss on the first date

Think positive

You can lead a horse to water but you can't make him drink

There's no free lunch

Don't throw the baby out with the bath water

It ain't over 'til it's over

A penny saved is a penny earned

A place for everything and everything in its place

Don't cry over spilled milk

Don't hide your light under a bushel

Less is more

His bark is worse than his bite

This too shall pass

Tomorrow's another day

Absence makes the heart grow fonder

Don't get in over your head

Beauty is only skin deep

Haste makes waste

The sky's the limit

Leave no stone unturned

Don't let the bastards get you down

EXPLANATION & COVER LETTER

When I started this book I wrote out a five-page questionnaire that I ended up mailing or handing out to about 130 people of retirement age that I know. Each had a code number so when I was reading them I wouldn't automatically know who had answered what. My plan was to write the book, then read the answers. If I found something that was pertinent or an interesting vignette on one of the subjects I would use it. And if I needed additional substance then I could look up who wrote it and ask for more information.

The last thing I was interested in was prying into my friends' private lives. In spite of my efforts, I got into trouble with the questionnaire and probably lost a few friends. One elderly woman said to me, "Why are you writing a book anyway? Who cares? Let people do what they want". I couldn't answer any of that and she definitely wasn't interested in any other thoughts of mine. And she is certainly entitled to her opinion. She didn't deter me although I was quite shaken by her vehement response.

I have added the cover letter and the questionnaire to the end of the book. If you would like to fill it out, be my guest. You know there will be no code number and my signature will not be at the end. You may send it or any letter to the publisher and they will forward it to me. Maybe I'll do a revised edition/sequel down the road with your ideas! Thanks!

HI GOOD FRIEND

Guess what? I'm going to try to write a book based on my experiences as a retiree. Several friends have suggested the subject and after giving it a lot of thought, I finally said, "what the hell, go for it". I don't have a title but I have a couple of ideas. How 'bout, Growing Up When You Retire or a bit catchier, How to Stay Young, Grow Up, and Have Fun When You Retire. It's only a beginning and I am wide open to a really catchy title. All suggestions carefully perused. OK?

The purpose of this letter is the enclosed questionnaire. I ask you, please, to take a little time to answer the questions as honestly as possible. My purpose is to talk about retirement for the future and to explore old and new options that people may not have thought of or are reluctant to investigate. What I'm looking for from you guys is one special thing to best illustrate a vignette or an idea in different and diverse areas. And hey, there are no wrong answers. All they are, are answers to various questions expressing different viewpoints and experiences.

One woman, Peggy from Portland, thought the questions were much too personal and probing and didn't want to be involved. She was the first person I showed the questionnaire to. Really shot me down. I hope you'll be more helpful. I really do want and need your feedback.

As I mentioned, the book is based on my experiences but my life is only mine. There are other ways and options and I hope to point these out to the many readers. I can't think of everything, so if you can help me out here, I will be more than grateful. What I want is to back up my opinions, suggestions and adventures with examples from friends from all over the country. Example: The husband of Kathleen, 80, left her 16 years ago for another woman. She was devastated, lost & totally lacking in self-esteem. Shortly after this, she met Steve who was 15 years younger. They have had a wonderful, fulfilling & non-sexual relationship that continues to this day. He dates others & she has self worth & contributes mightily to her community. A wonderful story of friendship!

I'm giving every questionnaire answerer a code number. I will give you credit (only if you wish) in the author's notes as consultants. I plan to throw away the envelopes and only use the code number for reference if I need to send you a reply and a further enlarged questionnaire. I really am not particularly interested in all these personal things but in my retired time, these various topics have come up in different experiences and conversations. Some of them to my amazement. So forgive me if you feel I am being too intrusive. I really don't mean to be. I do promise anonymity and my signature guarantees that.

Love and hugs gratefully, Lou

QUESTIONNAIRE

Code:

Year of birth: Age now: Level of education:

Gender: Age at retirement:.   State of residence:

1. Do you live in the same place you lived before you retired?
    Why?

    Did you ever think of moving away?
       Why did or didn't you?

    Do you think it is too late to change your mind?
       Why?

    What is or was your criteria for choosing a new location or staying in the same place?

2. Are you married? If yes, do you tell him/her everything?
    Why?

    How many new friends have YOU made since you retired?
       How did you meet ?

Are they special/best friends or maybe more like acquaintances? Why?

Do you have a BEST friend? or almost best? Same sex or opposite?

What is the appeal of this person?

How did you meet?

What & who made the friendship work?

If you want to make new friends, do you agree that "if you do what you like to do, you will meet people also doing what they like to do and maybe make a new friend"?

Has this happened to you? How?

Describe your social life. Busy? So-so? Dull? Perfect? How & why?

3. Do you have ample money to live on?
    Do you have a budget?

Are you able to stick to it?
> What happens when you don't?

Do you get stressed?
> In what way & what happens?

4. Have you worked since you retired?
> Why?

What kind of job?

Was it offered to you or did you seek it?
> Do you like it?   Why?

How long do you plan to do this?
> Why?

Is the pay commensurate with your abilities & experience?

5. Have you ever lived alone?   When & why?

Did you like it? How & why?

Have you ever eaten dinner in a restaurant alone?
Have you ever been to a movie, symphony, play, concert, etc. alone?
What was it & how did you feel the first time?

6. Do you do volunteer work? Where?

How long?   How often?
Have you done others before or even at the same time?
Do you like it?   Why?

Have you made new friends that will continue after the "work" is over?

7. Do you still buy the kinds of clothes you wore before you retired?   Why?

Have you changed your styles?   In what way?

Do you dress like your mother/father did?
Are you more "today"?   Why?

Do you shop a lot?   What kind of stores?

8. What subscriptions do you have?

What do you actually read?

With whom do you discuss what is happening here, there, & everywhere?

What do you do for entertainment?
How often?   And with whom?

9. What did you weigh in high school?
       in your 20's?   in your 30's?

And what do you weigh now?
Do you have a plan for keeping trim & healthy?
What is it?

Do you exercise?   Regularly?   What?

Do you walk regularly?

Do you like spectator sports?
Do you participate regularly in a personal sport?

What is your general health?
Do you have any continuing problems? Ailments?

What are they & how have they hampered you?

10. Have you had sex in the last 10 years?
   Regularly?   How often?

   Do you use Viagara?   Lubricants?
   Does it all work?

   How?

   Do you miss the old days & ways?
   Are you content?   Is your mate?

   Has there been a new person in your sex life?

   How has that made you feel?

11. Your additional comments.

All of the above and preceding pages are private & confidential.

Printed in the United States
36439LVS00008BA/79-90